D0497952

ANCIENT WISDOM –
MODERN INSIGHT

QUEST BOOKS

are published by
The Theosophical Society in America,
a branch of a world organization
dedicated to the promotion of brotherhood and
the encouragement of the study of religion,
philosophy, and science, to the end that man may
better understand himself and his place in
the universe. The Society stands for complete
freedom of individual search and belief.
In the Theosophical Classics Series
well-known occult works are made
available in popular editions.

Cover design by Kathy Miners

ANCIENT WISDOM – MODERN INSIGHT

Shirley Nicholson

This publication made possible with
the assistance of the Kern Foundation

The Theosophical Publishing House
Wheaton, Ill. U.S.A.
Madras, India/London, England

A Quest original. First edition 1985.
No part of this book may be reproduced in any manner without written permission except for quotations embodied in critical articles or reviews. For additional information write to:

The Theosophical Publishing House, 306 West Geneva Road, Wheaton, Illinois 60189.

A publication of the Theosophical Publishing House, a department of the Theosophical Society in America.

Library of Congress Cataloging in Publication Data
Nicholson, Shirley J.
    Ancient Wisdom.

    "A Quest original" — Verso t.p.
    Bibliography: p.
    Includes index.
    1. Theosophy.   I. Title.
BP65.N53A53   1985   299'.934   84-40513
ISBN 0-8356-0595-7

Printed in the United States of America

To F.L.K. who taught us by appealing to experience and by pointing to theosophy in the main currents of modern thought as well as in ancient streams.

About the Author

Shirley Nicholson is senior editor in charge of Quest Books for the Theosophical Publishing House. A life-long student of theosophy, she has lectured and taught classes on its various aspects for many years. She was a student of F. L. Kunz, founder of the Foundation for Integrative Education, and served as source reader for *Main Currents in Modern Thought*, the journal for the Foundation. A former teacher and counselor, Mrs. Nicholson is a Phi Beta Kappa graduate of the University of California at Los Angeles and has done graduate work in education.

Contents

Foreword

Down the ages, myths and legends have hinted at a great mystery. This is the existence of an Ancient Wisdom, hard to find, but offering great reward to the successful seeker. In modern times the situation is similar, except that the hints have swollen to a library of books about this Ancient Wisdom and guides towards seeking it. But for most people it still remains secret.

To discover why this is so, we may well consider the book of a modern seeker, Geoffrey Ashe. His book is called *The Ancient Wisdom: A Quest for the Source of Mystic Knowledge*. Since Ashe is a skeptical, logical, literal individual, his quest started by questioning even the existence of an Ancient Wisdom. He sought evidence in myths and books. He brushes aside much of H.P. Blavatsky's *Secret Doctrine* because it is (in his words) "a huge, shapeless amateurish book, often obscure," though "it has features which inspire respect." In the course of some 150 pages, Ashe manages to convince himself that there really *is* something to discover. He examines the significance of the number seven in myths and scriptures, and he locates the source of this "magic seven" in the mythical Shamballa, somewhere in Central Asia. He even offers two UFO events to support this conclusion, presenting a disproved theory with regard to one. However, he gives no real clue as to the *nature* of the Ancient Wisdom. So despite a long and scholarly investigation, Ashe never did find whatever it was that he was seeking nor how it arose, beyond establishing its reality and its original geographical location.

The Ancient Wisdom never will be discovered by any such logical approach. To the hard and the hard-headed, who prize the rational mind as the ultimate achievement of human evolution, it must remain forever secret. It can only be apprehended by those able to transcend personal emotions and thought processes, by those who are graced by intuition and mystical experience. As the author of this present book puts it: ". . . a search for the deeper wisdom must go hand in hand with a wholesome, ethical life. This kind of understanding cannot be won only on an intellectual level. It must involve the whole person at all levels of his being."

It may be said with some truth that the Ancient Wisdom was revealed in the Mystery Schools of antiquity. But what was taught was only the ways to prepare oneself to receive such grace, by self-purification, control of mind and emotions, and meditation. Such personal instruction has probably been available through the ages in secret societies, even during the Dark Ages. During this century, personal guidance has been offered to members of the Theosophical Society and more recently through many other bodies. For those prepared to work alone, guidance is now freely available through books on yoga.

Exoterically, the Ancient Wisdom is a body of arcane knowledge that may now be studied by any who are interested. The key source is the rather formidable volumes of *The Secret Doctrine* by H.P. Blavatsky, but many simpler accounts have since been published, culminating in this book. But esoterically the Ancient Wisdom is the *Source* of all this knowledge, only available to those who can transcend normal levels of consciousness and flip over into a new state of being in which one knows by becoming. This is Samadhi, Cosmic Consciousness, or the mystical experience. In the author's words: "As we quiet time's flow, we glimpse our roots in the timeless One." Thus we enter a monistic state of union with the One, in contrast to normal dualistic learning of knowledge regarded as external to oneself. The Secret Wisdom is not kept secret out of perversity, or from fear of misuse. It remains secret only because it is utterly inaccessible to anyone who has not made himself ready to receive it. Moreover, when a seeker *is* ready, a teacher is no longer needed. The Wisdom will arise of itself within his inner being.

Since it is impossible to convey this Wisdom in its fullness by the spoken or written word, it may well be asked: What is the use of writing still another book about it? The short answer is "to encourage others." Having been granted this enlightenment, even for a brief moment only, the joyous recipient may feel an irresistible urge to help others towards this same unimaginable blissful consummation. The right technique is not so much telling as evoking. Telling can only be done in hints and analogies, but these can be new, never used before. Who knows—what one writes may be just the trigger that awakens someone to this inner Vision, while nothing he has read hitherto has worked this magic. As the author says: "Words . . . can point the way, but for true insight they must be known experientially and lived out."

Nearly a decade ago, I felt such an urge myself. The theosophical "teachings" ought to be presented afresh, in modern language, supported by such recent discoveries in science and philosophy as point to these same eternal truths. I envisaged this as a joint effort, compiled by perhaps a dozen theosophical researchers pooling their individual understanding of the principles, each tackling one aspect of the whole. We might draw upon our own introspections, and perhaps discover inspiration from common sayings invested with previously hidden meaning. So I publicized the project in theosophical journals, appealing for contributions. But alas, the response was disappointingly meager: my inspiration failed to fire others with the same enthusiasm. Anyhow, books compiled by a group of authors are seldom satisfactory; they tend to remain a juxtaposition of individual essays that fail to amalgamate, unless the editor has the energy to rewrite every contribution in his own style. I did not feel equal to writing the whole book myself, so the project had to be dropped.

Now I am delighted to discover that Shirley Nicholson has written just such a book as I had envisaged—while in the meantime it happens that I have written two quite different and more specialized books myself. So I offer a heartfelt welcome to *Ancient Wisdom—Modern Insight*. We can turn gratefully from one project with a misconceived objective and another that never took off to one that promises to be a splendid success.

The book is based firmly, though not slavishly, upon *The Secret Doctrine*. Salient material has been selected, completely reorganized, and rewritten in the author's own words. The outcome is a crisp and eminently readable restatement of theosophical principles. There are three main sections, each divided into a number of chapters, sixteen in all; these are in turn conveniently split into several subdivisions. Obviously any author must think hard about his material, chapter by chapter. In this book the thinking is enlivened by intuitive insight; each chapter comes through as a deep meditation upon its theme.

The serious reader would be well advised to repeat this process, absorbing the book slowly in easy stages. That is to say, read only one chapter at a sitting (or even just one subdivision), then read it again. Meditate upon it for a time at least as long as that required for the reading. The meditation need not be a stiffly formal discipline; it may well be broken to refer back to the book. Some chapters merit continuing the meditation on the following day. In this fashion, a newcomer to the subject could gain a thorough grasp of theosophical principles (in the broadest sense) from this single book, by devoting to it, say, one hour a day for a month. Such an approach should stimulate the reader towards his own insights —and this is the object of the exercise. It is *not* to memorize the book, or to gain a coldly intellectual appraisal of its subject matter. It is to impress upon the mind not the *words* of the book but one's own individual understanding of them, using heart and intuition combined with thinking.

If I may presume to supplement the book, I should like to re-emphasize two themes from recent publications. The first is that some highly eminent scientists have committed themselves to a belief in a Cosmic Intelligence guiding the creation and development of the Universe. I would mention especially Sir Fred Hoyle, who wrote a book actually entitled *The In-*

telligent Universe, and Jim Lovelock who devotes his attention specifically to the Earth, and its guidance by a kind of Logos of the Earth, to which he gives the name of the Greek goddess Gaia.

The second theme is the phenomenal growth of all these ideas throughout the world, on something approaching a logarithmic scale. It used to be said that the salvation of our troubled Earth depended upon practical idealists. It is becoming realistic to go further and say that it depends upon practical mystics—and they are now arising in their thousands.

E. LESTER SMITH, D.Sc.
Fellow of the Royal Society

Preface

Since 1888 when H. P. Blavatsky's fountain source of esoteric philosophy, *The Secret Doctrine,* burst upon the learned world, any number of books on various aspects of its doctrines have appeared. There are deep and difficult expositions as well as simple ones easy to understand. Some are worked out logically and clearly and appeal to the rational mind, while some are more poetic and symbolic and appeal to the intuition. Amid this wealth of theosophical and esoteric literature, what can another book on theosophy contribute?

There are two considerations I feel need more emphasis, points which have appeared in other books but which to me have not been made sufficiently clear as important to our understanding of theosophy in the 20th century. First, I think theosophical ideas can be connected more broadly with developments in contemporary thought and thus shown to be highly relevant in today's world. Second, I wish to convey my conviction that these ideas, abstract though they may at first appear, are realities in nature and in ourselves that we can come to experience firsthand, at least in part.

As a student of theosophy for well over three decades, I have seen the thought of the world open more and more to ideas of the perennial philosophy. It seems that in every field alongside continuing materialism can be found strains of the Ancient Wisdom, from business to animal welfare, from medicine to rituals, but especially in science. A kind of spiritualization appears to be infusing modern thought. This trend is still in the forefront of today's culture, certainly not yet accepted by the majority. However, in a time when words like *holism* and *karma* have become part of ordinary speech, when scientists are juxtaposing physics and mysticism, when millions practice meditation, I cannot help being impressed at how pervasive certain ancient ideas have become.

It has not been easy to assimilate these newer trends into theosophical literature. There have been few writers who have perceived and articulated the age-old principles appearing in new guise. For, as F. L. Kunz made clear in the 1940s and 1950s, it is with the *principles* of theosophy, the sweeping metaphysical ideas, that juncture can be made with modern thought, not so easily with the details and specifics. Some such linkages have appeared but more often in articles and seminars than in books.

Therefore, I have organized this book around some major themes, overarching concepts, that keep reappearing, particularly in *The Secret Doctrine*. I have tried to explain these grand ideas and where possible to back them up with modern knowledge, especially science. Though the principles themselves are not dependent on any new developments and stand as eternal truths to those who know, it is still helpful to observe them where they coincide with modern thought.

I am not myself a scientist or specialist in any field except perhaps in theosophical studies, but over the years I have tried to some extent to keep up with the changing world of thought. I write as a theosophical student linking the Ancient Wisdom with modern developments where possible, trying to present the ancient truth in a 20th-century context. I refer to this perennial philosophy as *theosophy* with a lowercase *t* to indicate its universal character, as a reminder that these ideas are not limited to literature that came out in the late 19th and 20th centuries in theosophical and esoteric movements, but rather are to be found in innumerable sources, both ancient and modern. It is my hope that this endeavor will help some modern-minded people to assimilate the perennial truths of theosophy and also help some theosophists come to appreciate how modern and relevant the ancient doctrines really are.

My second reason for writing this book is to contribute what I can to showing that a deep study of theosophy need not be arid or just intellectual. Throughout history there have been sages and initiates who have discovered the reality behind esoteric teaching, the truths in nature that underlie the verbal expression. While we may not be able to remove the veil of language completely, anyone so inclined can grow in perception of these truths, so that at least some of his or her knowledge comes alive, becomes real. These eternal ideas have an energy, a vitality that enlivens those who probe them. They can lead to a wider experience of nature and its supporting spiritual background, a new vision of reality. Such a growing world view, far from being just an exercise in thought, can penetrate to all levels in us and reshape and transform us. The genuine student keeps growing in understanding, in sensitivity, in compassion, and in skills and ability to be of use in the world.

If this book succeeds in some measure in showing theosophy in the light of these two objectives, it will help repay my debt to the many companions on the way and mentors who have helped me to see theosophy as a living reality in my life and in the world.

I want to thank Emily Sellon, former editor of *Main Currents in Modern Thought*, Prof. Robert Ellwood, and Prof. John Alego for reading the manuscript and making invaluable suggestions. My thanks also go to Prof. Ralph Hannon who checked and made corrections in the discussions on science, and to Dr. E. Lester Smith for his foreword.

The Living Tradition

> Rudiments of the Perennial Philosophy may be found among the traditionary lore of primitive peoples in every religion of the world, and in its fully developed forms it has a place in every one of the higher religions. A version of this Highest Common Factor . . . has been treated again and again.
>
> Aldous Huxley, *The Perennial Philosophy*

*T*here comes a time for most of us when we begin to question the value of our lives, of our activities and achievements, even of ourselves. This may be a momentary quavering which we brush aside as merely a pessimistic mood, or it may be a prolonged and serious examination. But if we take the time to step aside from our lives and our habitual thoughts and feelings and look at them objectively, most of us will feel some dissatisfaction, that something is missing, that there must be more than this. Such unsettling moments of questioning often give birth to a "divine discontent," a hunger for something more, that gives us the impetus to discover new dimensions to life. Uncertainty, even despair, can shake us into a new mode, a new way, a search for meaning. Einstein sensed something of this as he glimpsed the immensity of the universe:

> The individual feels the futility of human desires and aims and the sublimity and marvelous order which reveal

1

themselves both in nature and in the world of thought. Individual existence impresses him as a sort of prison and he
wants to experience the universe as a single significant
whole. [This is] the beginnings of cosmic religious feeling.[1]

We may begin our search for cosmic religion, for our place
in the whole, by reading widely and examining many new
ideas and viewpoints, or our quest may lead us to explore
inwardly, to uncover new and deeper layers of our own consciousness through meditation and self-examination. Seeking
either outwardly or inwardly, we are likely to come across
ancient truths which have been unearthed by seekers through
the ages. We may be drawn into a philosophic vision that has
been with humanity since antiquity, a vision that has pointed
the way to human growth and wholeness.

The Ancient Wisdom

According to theosophical teachings, a few seers and sages,
geniuses of the inner life, have kept this secret teaching alive,
reiterating it in places scattered over the globe, at times that
span the range of history. This vision of man and his place in
the whole of things has been called esoteric philosophy, the
Perennial Philosophy, the primordial tradition, the Ancient
Wisdom, theosophy.

This network of ideas is called esoteric because it is concerned with that which is hidden, not obvious. It deals with
man's deeper structure concealed in the unconscious part of
his nature and the unseen processes and laws that stand
behind what is obvious to the senses. Genuine esoteric
philosophy is not concerned with the weird or uncanny,
though it may afford a rationale for such things. Its primary
focus is on the universal laws governing human evolution and
all natural phenomena, the principles that underlie the ob-
servable universe.

There have been times when the Ancient Wisdom was
taught only secretly to an inner circle of the few who sought
deeper truths. Though its teachings come alive to the mind
steeped in sincere inquiry, they have little meaning to the
superficial mind. Esoteric philosophy unlocks a view of real-

ity that goes beyond surface appearances to penetrate their noumenal depths. The genuine esotericist knows nature as a vast organic whole of which the physical world is but the visible veil or sheath. He perceives that invisible realms contain the causal elements of all being, producing in the outer sphere that which is perceptible to the senses. Thus, his vision is open to vast realms beyond the physical world.

Understanding the Ancient Wisdom, which has been called "a liberating whiff of reality," goes deeper than mental cognition. Words and verbal teachings can point the way to the hidden doctrines, but for true insight they must be known experientially and lived out. A few genuine adepts—such as Jesus, Buddha, Plato, Lao Tzu, and Pythagoras—have revealed the secret teachings through the ages. These sages embodied the wisdom in themselves and their lives. For them the life and the philosophy were of one piece; they illustrated that a search for the deeper wisdom must go hand in hand with a wholesome, ethical life. This kind of understanding cannot be won only on an intellectual level. It must involve the whole person at all levels of his being. For example, in the Greek mystery schools such as that of Pythagoras, mathematics was taught as a spiritual discipline in the context of his cosmology, such as the Music of the Spheres, and only to those who qualified both intellectually and morally. Thus science, religion, and philosophy were united with one another and with morality.

Other mystery schools such as the Eleusinian set the stage for direct participation in events dramatized to invoke realization of a secret teaching. Initiations were meant to bring about openings of the seeker's insight. The Masons and Alchemists, along with many other esoteric schools through the ages, offered training for the awakening of inner vision. Pythagoras, Plato, Roger Bacon, Kepler, Leonardo da Vinci, Nicolas of Cusa, and Leibnitz were among those said to have belonged to an esoteric school.[2]

There have been times when theosophical doctrines have been taught openly and publicly. The ancient Indian teachings recorded in *The Upanishads* were originally secret.[3] However, the central theme found in these teachings has been repeated in any number of exoteric writings. For example, "Tat tvam asi" (Thou art That), which proclaims man's inmost being as one with divine Being, or Brahman, is identical with the Gnostic maxim, "Thou art I and I am thou." This insight into man's hidden connection with the Ground of all has appeared in many other philosophies and religions, such as Taoism and Neoplatonism, and is even hinted at in Buddhism, though in a less explicit form. Esotericism holds that the direct realization of this truth is the highest achievement.

Recurrent Motifs

The fundamental polarity between divinity and the conditioned outer world is another matter for direct realization to the esotericist. This understanding of dual aspects of both man and nature appears in Hinduism as the poles of Brahman and maya, the illusory world, in Buddhism as nirvana and samsara, in Christianity as the contrast between the divine and human nature, in shamanism as the supreme Sky God and the world which he creates and then withdraws from.

Polarity and unity of all with the divine are only two examples of the many recurrent motifs found in the world's collective wisdom. The founders of all great religions taught some aspect of the Ancient Wisdom, and there remain strains of it at the heart of all living religions, though too often buried by misinterpretations which have accumulated through the ages. A knowledge of the esoteric tradition can make any religion more meaningful and understandable. Frithjof Schuon, authority on religious studies, makes it clear in his seminal work *The Transcendent Unity of Religions* that religious truth cannot have only one expression to the exclusion of others. To him a dogmatic affirmation that admits no other form of expression is like a point on a circle; it misses the fullness of truth.[4]

The inner teaching has been compared to a golden thread running through the tapestry of religion and philosophy. Jacob Needleman, who perceives philosophy as something living and relevant today, has pointed to "an ancient current of great, awakening ideas."[5] These recurrent ideas have appeared in different guises at different times through the centuries, expressed through many cultural colorings. Living truth cannot be static and must be seen anew as it relates to each new era. Yet esoteric teachings throughout history have a remarkable similarity. As philosophy professor Renée Weber recognizes, there is a single tradition, one universal core of knowledge underlying its many expressions, which are "bound by a common intentionality, an integral vision of man and world."[6] Though from innumerable times and places, these teachings point up certain basic principles and laws which are universal. They embody a holistic system which blends science, philosophy, and religion, as once they were merged in ancient Greece and the Orient. Theosophy reveals the ancient, narrow way for man to unfold the mystery of his inner nature and evolve to high and richer states of consciousness.

The Secret Doctrine

Helena Petrovna Blavatsky, the most insightful and comprehensive teacher of esoteric philosophy in modern times, stated and developed the basic principles of theosophy at the end of the 19th century in her seminal work *The Secret Doctrine.* There she cited sources and sages from all eras, as well as contemporary thinkers. She referred to this perennial philosophy as "the accumulated Wisdom of the ages" and emphasized its many sources: "The system . . . is no fancy of one or several isolated individuals . . . it is an uninterrupted record, covering thousands of generations of Seers."[7] She made it clear that she did not invent theosophy but merely brought its strands together into a harmonious whole, supplied the string for the bouquet, as she put it. She proclaimed that the basic conceptions of *The Secret Doctrine* "are, in fact, contained—though too often under a misleading guise—in every system of thought or philosophy worthy of the name."[8] She further stated that:

> In every age, under every condition of civilization and knowledge [are found] the more or less faithful echoes of

one identical system and its fundamental traditions—so
many streams of the same water must have had a common
source from which they started.[9]

Her work is the foundation for the proliferation of esoteric
teachings so popular today. Though published around a hundred years ago, *The Secret Doctrine* continues to be the main
source of the concepts and principles that make up the Ancient Wisdom. In it the fundamentals are intertwined with
esoteric lore. But, unlike many later writers, H.P. Blavatsky
always stressed and came back to the universals which
underlie and govern the universe. She revealed a comprehensive system of interlocking principles, a metaphysics, which is
the foundation of the manifested world. For example, she emphasized cycles as a principle rather than reincarnation, an
instance of the greater law, and repeatedly stressed evolution
as an omnipresent reality which subsumes the specifics of the
stages of development. She sketched the large picture, showing us the grand design behind our world of experience. Later
writers tended to fill in details and describe the mechanisms
involved in the outworkings of the principles.

Principles as Living Realities

These essentials are more accessible and easier to cor-
roborate in our own experience than the more detailed
teachings about superphysical worlds. Much of the esoteric
information available today is based on investigations by
gifted researchers with supernormal sensitivities into nature's
unseen realms. Information of this kind rests on the authority
of these individuals. The principles, however, can become
evident to anyone who searches in the right way, for understanding principles does not depend on any special ability
other than that of intuitive insight, which can be cultivated by
study and contemplation.

The fundamentals of theosophical metaphysics are not distant abstractions which have no effect on our lives. Rather,
they are at work all around us and within us here and now.
They are like gravity, which though unseen yet determines
the nature of the physical world. Everything we do is com-

pletely pervaded by the pull of gravity. Our every step and movement, each object we use, whatever we build or lift is dominated by this principle. Yet, because it is so pervasive and ever-present, we are usually unaware of the power of its influence. The grand principles of theosophy—unity, polarity, cycles, order, evolution—are also constantly exerting their irresistible influence in our world. As a contemporary theosophist put it: "Theosophical doctrines, the theorems of esoteric traditions, are not abstractions beyond the reach of most . . . but are as immediate and real as one's next breath or step on the path."

This knowledge has reappeared through history partly because it was repeatedly imparted from master to pupil through verbal teachings and initiations into its mysteries. But it is kept alive also because it is self-evident truth to those who have unlocked the secrets of nature for themselves. As a great sage once said: "These theories [are] unimpeachable facts to those who know."[10] As in the ancient mystery schools, these metaphysical ideas expressed in modern theosophy were not meant to be studied intellectually only and believed as articles of faith. This may be a start, but knowledge which remains intellectual has little effect on the world or the individual. Belief without knowledge can degenerate into dogma. These teachings are meant to be transformed from theories to living realities which permeate all our attitudes and govern our life. As H.P.B. (as she came to be known) says of the Stanzas of Dzyan, which form the basis of The Secret Doctrine, ". . . all these Stanzas appeal to the inner faculties rather than to the ordinary comprehension of the physical brain."[11] Deep contemplation of the universal principles and the ways they are woven together can awaken faculties deeper than ordinary comprehension—the higher mind and the intuitive faculty of direct and immediate perception. This is a natural process by which knowledge is turned into experience, "head learning" into "Soul wisdom," as H.P.B. put it, in which ideas are illuminated by a kind of living truth. The result is "vision-based organic knowledge as opposed to reasoned-out theory."[12]

The source of this new dimension of understanding is latent

in each of us. We can know the universals, the oneness behind all life, for such knowledge lies within us already, waiting to be actualized. As Krishna Prem, 20th-century commentator on *The Secret Doctrine,* put it, the philosophy behind the Stanzas, the *Gita,* the *Vedas* "draws its authority . . . from its own inherent truth as a description of and guide to the inner life, a truth which is testified to and guaranteed by our own hearts and our own hearts alone."[13] It is possible to find a level within ourselves where theosophy is reality and to allow its implications to permeate our minds, so that our lives come to express its principles.

For many of us in the Western world, the first step will be intellectual. First we may study, read, listen to lectures, discuss, as we consider and try to comprehend the ideas of theosophy. Then, if we are earnest in our search, this mental consideration should initiate a process within us. We begin to meditate on ideas which we have mastered intellectually and to "realize them in the mind," as H.P.B. said. At deeper levels of understanding, a kind of certainty dawns. In *The Transcendent Unity of Religions* Schuon describes a stage in which we no longer question the validity of an idea or look for proof of it. Neither do we simply believe it or rest on intellectual conviction. Rather we *know* its truth for ourselves; we have "direct evidence . . . that implies absolute certainty."[14]

As our understanding grows, we slowly begin to view the world from the perspective of theosophy, to see its principles at work below the surface of things, and to find evidence of cycles, evolution, higher planes all around us. We may also see more and more ways in which these ideas relate to our daily lives. They may begin to reflect in our emotions too, as new levels of love and compassion and the desire to serve. Thus, we ground these principles in experience and in our inner life so that they affect us at every level. As this process deepens, we may find that our attitude toward life is changing. We may become more able to remove ourselves from the limitations of our immediate situation and see its meaning from a broader perspective, from a more long-range view, as we look to larger goals. Thus, this process of turning ideas into experience engages our whole being. What starts as intellectual comprehension grows into intuitive insight and becomes grounded in practicality. Our faculties at all levels become focused on the quest, and we become involved in an unending process of growth, continually creative and fresh, that will go on year after year. We discover for ourselves that a true encounter of the self with the esoteric vision has the power to transform us.

I

The Many-Faceted One

1

The Healing World View

> We live today in a globally interwoven world, in
> which biological, psychological, social and environ-
> mental phenomena are all interdependent. To
> describe this world appropriately, we need an eco-
> logical perspective . . . a new paradigm—a new vi-
> sion of reality.
>
> Fritjof Capra

*A*n unearthly hush falls all around. Birdsong fades and
there are no small animals scurrying about. Traffic is all
but stopped, and people stand about quietly gazing skyward.
Though it is nearly noon, the cloudless sky darkens and the
remaining light takes on an eerie yellowish tinge. Silence and
darkness deepen until the world seems plunged into an un-
timely twilight. All life seems to stand still. Then, almost
imperceptibly, the yellow light creeps back, gradually bright-
ening. Soon the sounds of nature begin to hum and people
once more move about in their usual daily activities. The
world comes back to life and resumes its normal pace.

We have all occasionally experienced an eclipse of the sun
like this. Such dramatic natural events are not so frightening
to today's city dweller. But they were awesome to peoples
who lived close to nature, particularly in prescientific eras. A
tribesman with shamanistic beliefs, terrified at such a show
of the power of his gods, would perform sacrificial rites to

propitiate them and protect himself. A devout farmer might fall on his knees in prayer or light a candle to the Virgin in hopes that his crops would not be damaged. By contrast, a modern businessman might only glance at the sky briefly in his rush between important appointments, while his teen-age son might get the globe, a tennis ball, and a flashlight to show his little brother the positions of earth, moon, and sun during an eclipse. An astronomer would have prepared in advance to take telescopic pictures for studying the sun's corona, glowing around the dark disk of the moon.

The way each person reacts depends on his belief system. Different world views generate different interpretations of the same events. Is nature seen as permeated by invisible spirits, sometimes helpful, sometimes hostile, or is there a single benevolent God at work behind the scenes? Is the world focused on commerce in which nature is involved only indirectly? Is there an orderly celestial system in which heavenly bodies move in predictable ways? Each of these suppositions results in different attitudes and actions.

Our assumptions about the world screen our view like sunglasses, coloring our every experience, thought, belief, and attitude. These lenses are made of the fundamental premises and axioms we hold about nature and man, the "certainties" of life that we seldom question. Do we presume that physical life and sense experience are all there is? This view will reflect in the way we spend our time, the friends we choose, what is important to us. Do we feel people are basically good and that even behind seeming "evil" there is an urge toward growth and wholesomeness? This assumption will orient us differently and determine our life style, what we want to accomplish in life, and how we treat others.

Whatever its content, we all have a world view. We humans have a basic need for one. Anthropologists have found that all cultures embrace some sort of comprehensive vision of life which gives its members a sense of their place in the whole. Psychologists have found that individuals, too, require an overview by which they can orient themselves, what psychologist Erich Fromm has called a "frame of orientation."

What philosopher Jacob Needleman said of philosophy can also be said of world view:

> Man cannot live without philosophy . . . there is a yearning in the human heart that is nourished only by real philosophy.[1]

In a culture, as in an individual, the world view incorporates what is known from science at that time and place, plus religious and philosophical ideas. The predominant world view of the West today has grown up around 19th-century materialism, perhaps blended with newer ideas such as Relativity and Heisenberg's Uncertainty Principle. Even if we have not studied such concepts, they pervade our culture and affect our world view. Onto this cultural backdrop each of us inserts innumerable themes and motifs that fuse to make our individual picture of the world. That picture will include attitudes from early childhood which as adults we have largely forgotten—such as our reactions to quick or delayed feeding following our infantile cries of hunger, or our happiness or fright at encountering the family dog. These impressions will merge with more conscious, rational concepts in our image of the world.

The philosophical premises and root assumptions by which we live are largely unexamined; they just grow in our minds as we accumulate experience and knowledge. They are not thought through and formulated verbally in rational statements. Studies have shown that people become hostile and defensive when someone challenges such unconscious axioms. They make up what has been called "the philosophic unconscious"[2] of which we are largely unaware and therefore not prepared to defend. They are part of our being; we identify with them. When they are attacked, we feel we are attacked. Our world view, based on these premises, influences our experiences and actions far more than we realize, not only in highly charged moments like an eclipse but in daily life and habitual attitudes. What we believe the world to be like determines the way we interpret what happens to us, what we expect and what we think is expected of us, what we believe we can accomplish, even what we perceive ourselves to be.

The Separative World View

The world view prevalent today in the West has led to fragmentation, both of the world and in ourselves. Many authors have recently pointed out that this view rests on 19th-century Reductionism, which led to analyzing things into smaller and smaller constituents. Mind is seen as only a function of the brain, and consciousness is a byproduct of physical evolution. In this view the world takes on a thingness, a physicality, and seems to be made up of isolated, independent units which appear to be inherently disconnected.

As physicist David Bohm has pointed out, this kind of thought is one of the key factors in the divisive attitude which permeates the world today.[3] Our impulse to break up reality into fragments which we perceive through the senses is reinforced by language, which stresses differences. We see separate, discrete items—trees, chairs, buildings—and distinct people who appear to have an identity of their own, standing out as self-enclosed individuals. We invest these sense impressions of the world with far more significance and finality than they warrant, without realizing that there are other ways of experiencing our environment. Our "focal setting," as the Tibetan teacher Tarthan Tulku calls it, is restricted to one narrow angle. Einstein, too, saw this limitation we place on ourselves:

> Out of the multitude of our sense experiences, we take, mentally or arbitrarily, certain repeatedly occurring complexes of sense impressions . . . and we correlate to them a concept—the concept of bodily object.[4]

Today this divisive outlook is being questioned by many modern thinkers who are converging on an expanded vision of reality. This theme is beginning to appear as a major new thrust at the forefront of modern thought. Authors as diverse as the physicist Fritjof Capra and the authority on religions Huston Smith have pointed to signs that a new world view is emerging in Western culture. These thinkers show how advances in science, particularly regarding the nature of matter (discussed in chapter 4), make a divisive mind-set obsolete. Many students of sociology believe we are at a turning point, from the old atomistic, separative view to one which is holistic and focused on interconnections. There are many facts and theories in science that support such a view, some of which will be discussed throughout this book.

However, in spite of convincing evidence to the contrary, our deep-seated habits based on a separative vision of reality are hard to break. Our "philosophic unconsciousness" resists change, just because it is out of the realm of conscious awareness and choice. We have accepted separative concepts based on sense impressions as the final reality for so long that the boundaries they reflect have established themselves as inviolable. We respond to them as we do to the mime who makes us believe in an invisible wall which he creates with his gestures. We then limit ourselves to conform to the wall which we imagine to be there.

This separate view also pervades our concept of ourselves. Most of us in the West have grown up thinking of ourselves as distinct, independent persons in our own inner worlds. Even among the more enlightened of us, the strongest trend is to live in the midst of a self-centered sphere, holding our personal interests and benefits as of primary importance, our energies spent in enhancing our own private world, often at the expense of others. Our American ideals of individualism and competition are based on this view, which has served us well for most of our history. But now we are being forced to recognize our planet as a "global village" in which we cannot stand apart from others. Instant communication world-wide, global travel and trade, diminishing supplies of the world's resources, overpopulation are some of the well-known factors which should move us toward harmonious interconnectedness. Yet our emphasis on distinctions—between races, nations, ethnic groups, social classes, families, individuals—is preventing us from working together for the common good, and even for survival.

Toward Unity

More and more of us recognize that our failure to adopt the unitive attitude implicit in 20th-century knowledge is the basis of all our major problems world-wide, whether social, political, ecological, economic, or individual. Now at the end of the 20th century, more than ever before in history, we must realize that we cannot live isolated from one another and from nature. However, as long as we believe the world is divided into fundamentally separate units, we will experience the world in this way and react accordingly. But if we are convinced of an underlying unity behind the apparent divisions, we will experience unity and relatedness. We desperately need a unifying world view to help heal the world's endless fractures. What problems could not be solved by first considering the good of the whole, of the lives of all those on our planet, rather than special interests!

David Bohm tells us that modern physics reveals a view of matter in which "what we see immediately is really a very superficial affair . . . what we call the things that are real are actually tiny little ripples which have their place, but they

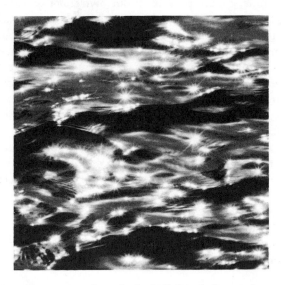

have been usurping the whole."[5] Behind the surface separation and supporting the seemingly disparate things is a unity more basic, more real, closer to us than our sense impressions, which always separate and can never reveal unity. Yet mystics agree with physicists that this unitary realm is primary, that the divisions ultimately rest on a unitary background. Our senses show us only the surface of the water. We are preoccupied with waves and eddies, splashes and sprays. If we could intuitively dive into the quiet depths, we would see the surface movements are only momentary, transient conditions of the abiding, dynamic whole.

Though difficult, it is possible to change our focal setting and perceive in ways other than the limited senses, to pierce into a more fundamental level. Throughout the ages there have been individuals who realized a background unity through immediate experience. Mystics from all religions have tasted union with the All in varying degrees. Today many ordinary people are also coming to experience some degree of direct encounter with this oneness through meditation and other means. The psychologist Stanislav Grof has discovered through clinical work that "it is becoming increasingly evident that humans can function in vast fields of consciousness, transcending the boundaries of their physical bodies, the range of their sensory organs, and the Newtonian characteristics of space and time."[6]

Psychiatrist Carl Jung reached a state of unity by immersing himself in nature:

> At times I feel as if I am spread out over the landscape and inside things, and am myself living in every tree, in the splashing of the waves, in the clouds and the animals that come and go, in the procession of the seasons.[7]

Erwin Schroedinger, founder of quantum mechanics, came to realize oneness by penetrating the nature of matter:

> Inconceivable as it seems to ordinary reason . . . —you and all other conscious beings as such—are all in all. Hence this life of yours which you are living is not merely a piece of the entire existence, but is in a certain sense the *whole* . . . .
> Thus you can throw yourself flat on the ground, stretched out upon Mother Earth, with the certain conviction that you are one with her and she with you.[8]

The Eastern yogi penetrates to an even deeper level of unity, in which he knows directly that he is one with the divine, that Atman and Brahman are one. This is the core discovery of mystics.

The key to this experience lies in the nature of man's basic being in the depth of his consciousness. The Ancient Wisdom has always held that each of us, like everything else in nature, is fundamentally one with the All, immersed in that undivided, numinous unity from which all creation springs. If we learn to open up to our own inner depths, "turning about in the deepest seat of consciousness," as the Buddha put it,[9] we can emerge in the realm of the One, just as physics, penetrating deep into matter, pierced into a world beyond materiality.

Arthur Koestler, a journalist who has explored mysticism, writes of the moral obligation that flows from the experience of union. This is not an experience merely for one's private expansion and enlightenment; rather, it engenders a sense of responsibility for others. While held prisoner in Fascist Spain with the possibility of being shot, Koestler had an experience in which "the I had ceased to exist," and he felt himself "floating on my back in a river of peace, under bridges of silence." In this state of being in touch with "real reality," as he put it, he came to a new realization:

> It struck me as self-evident that . . . we were all responsible for each other—not only in the superficial sense of social responsibility but because, in some inexplicable manner, we partook of the same substance of identity, like Siamese twins or communicating vessels.[10]

He perceived that the inner knowledge of unity must have outworkings in our lives. Another man of mystical inclination from a very different background, the Amerindian teacher and healer Sun Bear, came to the same realization: "We have to come to a point when we truly feel the oneness, the unity *in all the aspects of our lives*" (emphasis added).[11]

If enough of us can perceive the new view of wholeness emerging in our times and absorb it into our consciousness so that it permeates our world view, and hence our attitudes and actions, our new vision cannot help but reflect in world attitudes and conditions. As we ourselves become whole and live as intrinsic parts of the Whole, we can begin to re-establish wholeness in our tragically fragmented and divided world so full of crises. The mystic vision can begin to heal the world.

The esoteric philosophy of the ancients that H.P.B. represented over a hundred years ago rests on the principle of unity, of organic wholeness, strange and out of keeping with the 19th century but emerging forcefully today. Many aspects of theosophical philosophy have been corroborated by developments in modern thought; many theosophical ideas are "in the wind" today. The most pervasive and fundamental of these is the concept of unity, wholeness, organicity, ecology. Our times cry out for this unitive view. Yet, as we shall see, it has been available since before recorded history.

2

Interconnections

Nature has linked all parts of her Empire together by
subtle threads of magnetic sympathy, and there is a
mutual correlation between a star and a man.
Mahatma Letters

*T*he unity of all life—this is the foundation on which all
theosophical thought rests. All things are interconnected
and bound together as by an invisible thread. At every
level—from the atom and its parts through the myriad forms
of life to the farthest stars and galaxies—all is permeated by
one Life. Everything that exists emerged from the same unitary background, an unchanging Reality, which continually
supports and gives life to the whole cosmic process.

This is a staggering idea when we consider the vast diversity of forms in the universe. How can the endless variety of
things around us be one? What can bind the starfish, the
crystal, the moon, to ourselves, or ourselves to the African
Bushman or the Islamic sheik? How can a fragile, exquisitely
organized bird be related to the immense chaotic bursts of
energy in a quasar?

According to esoteric philosophy, everything that exists
stems from the "Rootless Root of all," a creative fountain
from which all life flows. In H.P.B.'s words, *"The Secret Doc-*

trine postulates the One Form of Existence as the basis and source of all things,"[1] and elsewhere she refers to "the divine unity from which all proceeds."[2] Our world of diversity, the many, emerges from the numinous Source of all, the One. Thus oneness is primary and fundamental in the theosophical view, and the separated things we experience in the world are secondary and rest on an unseen foundation of unity.

The Secret Doctrine holds that the One becomes the many through a process of emanation. "The One Existence breathes out a thought, as it were, which becomes the Kosmos."[3] Our world of myriad, separate forms solidifies gradually, by degrees, from its numinous unitary origin. From a passive state in which potentiality lies dormant, the world process stirs up the restless, unceasing activity we see around us.

> [The One Life] passes, at every rebirth of Kosmos, from an inactive state into one of intense activity that it differentiates.[4]

However, the world of materiality emerging out of the One

As water churns into foam, so the undifferentiated Source gives rise to the world.

is never in any way cut off from its divine Source. The esoteric view is in opposition to that of a God who creates the world and then steps aside from it. It also contrasts with materialism, which sees matter as inert and lifeless. Rather, the One Life permeates, supports, and gives life to everything that arises from it. The One Form of Existence manifests *in* matter; it is the "animating soul, immanent in every atom, latent in the stone, manifested in man,"[5] the "motivating, impelling potency" behind nature. Still, the One remains undivided as the homogeneous basis for widely different things, the ultimate essence that unites all the diversities in our seemingly pluralistic world. "Man . . . [and] the universe and all therein are one with the absolute Unity, the unknowable deific essence."[6]

There is another aspect of unity aside from the unitary essence in the depths of material things. There is a harmonious structure in the universe itself, as displayed by its parts, a wholeness revealed in relationships. Interactions, interdependence, coherence characterize the world of nature, in which separate beings and parts mesh together into meaningful patterns and wholes, as in the functions of the organs of the body. Thus, unity appears even when we focus on material manifestation rather than its underlying essence. H.P.B. refers to "the Non-Separateness of all that lives."[7] She presents a grand view of creation as an immense, interacting chain: "From *Gods* to *men,* from Worlds to atoms, from a star to a rush-light, from the Sun to the vital heat of the meanest organic being—the world of Forms and Existence is an immense chain, the links of which are all connected."[8] "The Great Chain of Being" graphically illustrates the unbroken unity behind the many individuals.

Thus theosophy points to three dimensions of unity: the undifferentiated unity of ultimate Being; the essence or life permeating all forms; the organic unity found in the harmony of parts and interactions in the world. We might symbolize the Ultimate Unity by a shoreless sea of light filling all space. The One Life within all forms might be represented by a lamp whose glow is powered by an invisible electric current. Parts structured into a harmonious whole could be likened to a masterful painting in which each element relates to and derives its meaning from the entire composition. These images might help illustrate how unity is forcefully present in the world and also lies at deeper levels behind the world.

Man and the One

We, too, are part of the One, never apart from the One Life. As children of Nature, we fit into her holistic patterning as we continuously exchange with and relate to the environment. We are an intrinsic part of the natural world. In addition, in the depths of our consciousness we are one with the Essence which permeates all, which is also our own inner being. In delving within in meditation to find the inmost self, the core of our own being, we somehow mysteriously merge with the supreme Self of all and for a time become conscious in some degree of our oneness with the divine life. H.P.B. quotes from an ancient scripture:

> In the Catechism, the Master is made to ask the pupil:
> "Lift thy head, O Lanoo; does thou see one or countless lights above thee, burning in the dark midnight sky?"
> "I sense one Flame, O Gurudeva, I see countless unde-tached sparks shining in it."
> "Thou sayest well. And now look around and into thy-self. That light which burns inside thee, dost thou feel it different in anywise from the light that shines in thy Brother-men?"
> "It is in no way different, though the prisoner is held in bondage by Karma, and though its outer garments delude the ignorant into saying, 'Thy Soul and My Soul.' "[9]

Such is the teaching that underlies the theosophical statements about the brotherhood of all people. Brotherhood is seen, not as ideal to be achieved, but as a reality in nature, an expression of the unity which pervades all life at every level. We can veil this unity with separateness and egoism, but this does not erase its roots deep in nature and in ourselves.

Support for the concept of interrelatedness is emerging from all sides. This idea, strange and foreign a hundred years ago, is becoming more and more important in modern thought. In recent decades, wholes rather than parts are becoming the focus. Studies of interconnections are yielding more understanding than looking at isolated bits reveals, and holistic, ecological world views are emerging from science itself. In the 20th century the world is beginning to appear as one undivided whole, its parts in intimate, dynamic relationship, flowing and moving rather than mechanical. There is overwhelming evidence from the most diverse sources that we are interconnected, that we are all part of one whole, sharing at all levels.[10] Perhaps the beautiful image of the whole earth with its swirling waters as seen from the moon can best symbolize the overall perspective that is emerging today.

Let us look at some examples of this principle reflected in the world through interconnections and harmonious relations. Later (in Chapter 6) we will consider the transcendent Source of the unity of nature. In these modern corroborations we can see the principle of interconnectedness as it actually operates within us and all around us. Considering these examples and modern views will also help bring more reality to our understanding of theosophy and the writings of H.P.B.

If we can learn about our interconnections and be convinced of their reality, we can come to experience unity for ourselves, so that the idea will take hold in us and grow creatively. We can then open ourselves to its influence in more and more ways, at all levels of our being, from harmony with a tree, to empathy with someone in distress, to intimations of one world, to mystical union with the All.

The Web of Life

We know that our bodies, which seem so personal, so distinctly our own, are also part of the universe. They are made of the same kinds of atoms found on the moon or in Alpha Centauri, and the elements we know on Earth as fundamental building blocks of all chemistry are the same to the farthest star of the most distant galaxy. Astronomers tell us that almost all the atoms in our bodies have been processed through supernova explosions in the distant past. The carbon in our cells, on which our life structure depends, was synthesized, not on earth, but in distant stars, as were other heavier elements. We are of the stuff of the universe.

Furthermore, these atoms and molecules in our bodies are by no means our private property. We take in countless millions of them continually and give back more millions to the environment. Atoms in our bodies now might well at one time have been in the body of Cleopatra or Confucius.

We are all caught in the grand cycle of circulation of the earth's materials. The same volume of water has existed on earth for millions of years. We know that millions of gallons of the life-sustaining liquid rise from rivers and seas in the form of water vapor. Some of this, condensed into tiny droplets, shows itself to us as clouds, from which raindrops plummet and snowflakes drift back to earth. These find their way into rivers and streams and seas, but along the way living things partake of the water, retain it for awhile, and return it to the cycle. As water continually flows in and out of us, we capture a constant amount to form the largest part of our cells before releasing it again into the endless flow. We share the very stuff of our bodies with all nature, in constant circulation.

In a similar way gases from the air flow in and out of us as we ceaselessly exchange atoms and molecules with the environment through our breathing. All living creatures share the atmosphere, as we see so dramatically when it becomes polluted. In addition, all living creatures share similar genes, and there are other signs of relationship, such as the close resemblance of enzymes of grasses to those of whales.

The ecologist John Storer is acutely aware of our interconnections. He says:

> Life is such a very personal thing, wrapped up within the being of every living creature, that it is sometimes hard to realize how intimately each life is connected with a great many other lives. Life is a flowing stream, forever passing away and as constantly being renewed. The energy that brings us life is supplied from many sources, most of them beyond our vision or experience.[10]

To biologists, who cannot perceive us as independent selves apart from our environment, our real selves are not confined within our skins but must include the entire environmental field.

A web of relationships shows up again and again in the study of ecological systems in which seemingly independent organisms form a single balanced harmonious system, individuals and species performing functions needed by the whole. For example, in the African savannah different species of animals graze at different levels of the vegetation, some on leaves of bushes, some on grasses, and so on. Predators hunting the different species seek different targets among the grazers. They have a pecking order so that some, like the lions, get first chance to kill, and even the vultures patiently wait their turn. The remains of the dead animals enrich the soil and in turn the grasses, as do the animal feces. Thus the microbes and insects that speed this breakdown form an essential strand in this intricate web. Each species in some way contributes to the overall balance of the system.

We, too, are woven into the web of life. We see the effects of our input in diminishing supplies of water and essential resources, in pollution of the air and water, and the defacement of the face of the planet. We know now that the choices we make in how we use the land affect all life, and it has become apparent in the 20th century that all living things in some manner are related to one another. Fairfield Osborn of the Conservations Foundations states it graphically:

> The youngster captive on the sidewalks of our big cities, the farmer struggling in the dust bowl, the sullen river that once ran silver, the desolate tangle of the second growth, even the last condor on a California mountaintop—all have a tenuous relationship to life on this earth as a whole. Man does not stand alone.[11]

The Family of Man

Nor can any of us stand apart from our fellows. We in the Western world take pride in our uniqueness as individuals, our personal differences. Yet even as we stand apart as individuals, we merge together as one family. Geneticists calculate that everyone on earth today is related to everyone else at least in the order of fiftieth cousins, that all the family trees of today's population merged into one in the not-so-distant past. Distinctions of race are insignificant as compared to the close kinship among us all. We all share the same pool of genes. Each of us has as ancestors Europeans, Africans, Chinese, Arabs, Malays, Latins, Eskimos, and every possible type of human being. Students of genetics are forced to believe in human brotherhood. Each of us is literally kin to humankind; we are all the family of man.

In addition to our physical similarities, we are moved and motivated by species-wide drives and needs, ranging from water to love, from food to self-esteem, from safety to mental stimulation. We require all these and more for complete health. Our ways of satisfying our needs are influenced by our social groups. Cows cannot serve as food to Hindus who revere them; insects which are delicacies to certain South American tribes are unpalatable to most of us. Our social groups profoundly affect what we are and bind us in a sphere of mutual influence. Families are such close-knit units that any disturbed member affects the whole family. Family therapists go so far as to view the one with the obvious problem as a symptom of the malfunctioning of the whole group, which they see as forming a field. They deal with relationships among all family members in order to help the problem child. We are so much part of our social groups—our schools, business organizations, communities, etc.—that it is impossible to study us in isolation. Anthropologist Gregory Bateson sees man's only real self as the total network of individual and society and environment.[12]

Jung has shown us that even our dreams are not ours alone. People the world over dream of heroes and princesses, witches and dragons, magic circles and mandalas. Mythological motifs of dreams and fairy tales are universal—" . . . fantasy images that are surprisingly alike and can be found practically everywhere in all epochs . . . "[13] These archetypes, as Jung called them, belong to the trend in us all toward common types of symbolic representations. They spring from a deep layer of consciousness below the purely personal, an image-producing stratum he called the *collective unconscious* or *objective psyche*. In this region of the mind we all express through universal symbols, uniting us in a species-wide language of the unconscious.

We constantly share and interact with each other on all levels. Though each of us is a unique individual, we make up one humanity, our divisions into groups and nations are less fundamental than our oneness. Through history we have identified with larger and larger units—first family and tribe, then leagues of tribes, city-states, nations, at first small, later including super-powers. Today some forward-looking idealists are beginning to open their focal setting wide enough to include the entire planet and feel themselves citizens of the world, with allegiance to all people everywhere, to the good of the whole human family. David Spangler, a visionary who is deeply concerned with community, is optimistic about this widening view:

> The vision of an emergent planetary culture involves the broadening and deepening of our individual and collective perspectives and assumptions so that we embrace ourselves as a species, as humankind, rather than as separate factions. It involves, moreover, seeing ourselves as sensitive, interdependent members of a community of life that transcends the human and embraces the whole of planetary ecology, including the Earth itself as a living being.[14]

In the theosophical perspective, as we have seen, every being is related to every other in an immense harmonious pattern, like an organism. In this view, isolation does not exist in any real sense, as even the tiniest life has an essential place in the overall structure.

Seeing Our Interconnections

Though we may give verbal and conceptual assent to this perspective, still it is hard to shift our focus to actually perceive it. We have for so long invested reality in the world of perception based on sense impressions. Through some miracle of our nervous system combined with consciousness, for eons we have received impressions from sight, sound, smell, touch, and somehow in the brain integrated them into discrete objects, and our language has solidified this discreteness. We get positive feedback from this operation because our "objects" are perceived by others as well. We can handle the objects, use them, eat them, hear them, and they seem to have a solid identity "out there." Our natural unconscious assumption is that discrete objects are real and our perception of the world based on them is accurate. From there we have built up a belief in separation, that we and the world consists of discrete self-enclosed entities.

At one level this assumption is correct, but if we change our focal setting, the world of discrete objects recedes. If instead of zooming in on individuals, we go the other way and take a wide-angle setting, we see systems, communities, solar systems, galaxies. Our interconnections take on a new reality and we begin to perceive ourselves in a context, in an ecological setting that grows until it includes the whole universe.

3

Holism and Hierarchy

> Individual reality is essentially illusory. Primarily, objects and events are part of a pattern which itself is part of a larger pattern, and so on until all is included in the . . . pattern of the universe. Individual events and objects exist, but their individuality is distinctly secondary to their being part of the unity of the pattern.
>
> Lawrence Le Shan

*E*verything contains or is penetrated by all other things. Those with the right kind of sensitivity can see into a reality of mutual penetration beyond the illusory realm of separation. Such is the vision of the Kegan school of Mahayana Buddhism. This view of reality is captured in a beautiful Buddhist image described by Ken Wilber: " . . . the universe is likened to a net of glittering gems, wherein each jewel contains the reflection of all other jewels, and its reflection in turn exists in all other gems: 'one in all, all in one.' "[1]

H.P.B. held, too, that we each connect with and carry within ourselves the whole of things:

> The Secret Doctrine . . . teaches that every one of the higher, as of the lower worlds, is interblended with our own objective world: that millions of things and beings are, in point of localization, around and *in* us as we are around, with and in them.[2]

This cryptic statement suggests something more than the harmonious integration of parts into wholes. It conveys the interpenetration of things, that entities do not stand apart and alone with a distinct, separate identity, but rather somehow occupy each other's space, mingle together and blend into one another, while still retaining their individual identity.

Interpenetration is one way to express the concept of hierarchy as developed in esoteric philosophy, that every entity lives its life in the field or sphere of a greater being. This applies in the sense that smaller beings are embedded in larger ones, as the "little lives" of our cells have their being in the life of the body, or the individuals in a nation are part of a national consciousness. This hierarchical principle is fundamental in theosophical philosophy, extending to the realm of great spiritual consciousnesses in which we "live and move and have our being."

Throughout nature, levels of organization can be found in which greater beings are composed of smaller and smaller ones, with all the levels interpenetrating and relating in every possible way, binding all together into an integrated whole. This hierarchical principle is a further expression of the interconnectedness of things in the Great Chain of Being, reflecting the all-encompassing principle of unity.

This concept of interpenetration, of universal connectedness, found in Eastern religion and esoteric philosophy, has reverberations in the modern perspective called *holism*. The concept of holism is discussed widely in the contemporary world in many diverse fields. It was first defined as a universal process by the philosopher-statesman Jan Smuts in 1920. It has been extensively developed by Ludwig von Bertalanffy, the noted biologist, and more recently by the Belgian Nobel Laureat Ilya Prigogine, who extended it to include principles of self-organization in living things.

The Holistic Perspective

Holism is not a well-defined theory but rather a unified, multilevel view which harmonizes many focal settings into one overall vision of unity. It stresses the interdependence and dynamic nature of systems and points to parallels, connections, and underlying unities. The British philosopher of science L. L. Whyte describes its hierarchical nature:

> The holistic view . . . regards the universe as a great hierarchy of unities, each following its own path of historical development. Each pattern, whether it is a crystal, an organism, a community, the solar system, or a spiral nebula, possesses its own internal order and is part of a more extensive order, so that the universe is recognized as a System of systems, a Grand Pattern of patterns.[3]

From this perspective we see all nature consisting of interlocking wholes. An organism—a tree or mouse or person —consists of complicated structures which are made up of complete units. The atoms of any body are whole, coherent, independent to a degree. They join to form molecules which again are complete and whole. These are organized into organelles (microscopic bodies within cells), organelles into cells, cells into tissues, then organs, then the systems which make up the biological organism. Each level of wholes is comprised of smaller wholes and at the same time serves as a part of larger wholes. Nature shows us nothing but wholes that are part of greater wholes. They form levels from simple to highly complex, each level connected with and interrelated to all other levels, forming multilevel structures, systems within systems.

These wholes are dynamic, constantly reconfiguring as changes at any level reverberate through the others. In biological systems we can see how patterns at higher levels regulate lower levels as molecules do more than interact with nearby molecules; they behave in ways that suit the needs of the organism. Conversely, cancer cells gone awry determine the fate of the entire organism. Lower levels feed into the dynamism of the whole system, even as higher levels impose their patterns.

Whole-making does not stop at the biological level. Organisms are part of a social whole; living things belong to families, communities, populations. Humans and other social animals form organized groups—colonies, bands, schools, business organizations, communities of all sizes and kinds.

A city like New York can be viewed as a giant organism. Input of sources of energy can be seen dramatically early in the morning when lines of trucks carrying goods for city-dwellers wait to pass through the tunnels into the city. Output of wastes is obvious during a garbage collection strike when mountains of refuse pile up on the streets. Output also flushes through sewers and rises into the atmosphere, where trees play their part in the system by obligingly absorbing many pollutants, as they release oxygen for the city's collective breath. At every level there are interconnections among a city's systems—such as the traffic flow system, the educational system, the economic system. A poor traffic system causes businesses to leave the city, which has an impact on the economic system; the result is less tax money for the school system, which then can produce fewer qualified workers for business. The mores, values, and life styles of various groups also affect the systems in many ways, both subtle and direct. The complex man-made unit of the city exhibits the principle of holism.

The perspective of holism (or wholism, as it is coming to be spelled) has outworkings in many fields today, the best known of which is health. In holistic health practices, the patient is seen as a living, whole person, rather than as the carrier of an illness disconnected from various other functions. Psychological and spiritual factors are as important as—even more important than—diet and hygiene in maintaining health. Therapy takes into account the patient's total orientation to life, not just illness localized in some part of the body.

Eminent thinkers from various fields have based world views on the perspective of holism. Joseph Needham, a philosopher of science, speaks of the integrity and wholeness of each individual as well as the interconnections between all one's parts. He explains that modern science with its philosophy of integrative levels and complete organisms has come around to the ancient Chinese world view:

> The harmonious cooperation of all beings arose, not from the orders of a superior authority external to themselves, but from the fact that they were all parts in a hierarchy of wholes forming a cosmic pattern, and what they obeyed were the internal dictates of their own natures.[4]

Teilhard de Chardin, a Jesuit paleontologist, was deeply convinced both from science and philosophy that the universe is whole, one piece. He saw it as a kind of gigantic atom that cannot be divided:

> The farther and more deeply we penetrate into matter, by means of increasingly powerful methods, the more we are confounded by the interdependence of its parts. Each element of the cosmos is positively woven from all the others . . . . *It is impossible to cut into this network to isolate a portion without it becoming frayed and unravelled at all its edges.* [5]

Many-Textured Relations

From the holistic perspective nothing can be seen in isolation; everything reflects and influences everything else. Plato's analogy of the world as a giant animal perhaps captures the essence of this view in which things interpenetrate in a complex way. Rather than rigid links strung together linearly, things are as they are because of interconnections at many levels, in many dimensions. This shows most dramatically in the development of personality. Any number of environmental factors and relationships impinging on the child have their influence in shaping his or her character, while the child in turn affects the surroundings.

Not only does everything reflect everything else in the immediate environment—there are connections with the whole world, with the universe. A war thousands of miles away or an explosion deep in outer space reverberates in our neighborhood, in us, and to some extent contributes to what we are. Alfred North Whitehead, a philosopher of science in the early 1900s, spoke of these connections:

> . . . the togetherness of things involves some doctrine of mutual immanence. In some sense or other, this community of the actualities of the world means each happening is a factor in the nature of every other happening . . . . We are in the world and the world is in us. [6]

Though we may often feel isolated and apart, we always have rich interconnections with the world, with people, at all levels of our being. We might transform our view of ourselves and the world if we could learn to train our focal settings on connections and cultivate ourselves in the spirit of oneness. Instead of stressing distinctions and the isolation of things, we can look at them as parts connected to form an organic whole. When we expand our consciousness and focus on this rather than on our seeming isolation, we can begin to live more fully, in a wider way.

Our imagination can carry us even farther. For example, as we enjoy something beautiful, we can also consider its inter-relations. A tree has roots deep in the earth which support it and draw water from deep sources, even as the leaves absorb energy from the sun. The tree exchanges huge amounts of gases with the atmosphere, absorbing carbon dioxide and pollutants, giving off water vapor, and refreshing the air with oxygen. It provides shade and homes for birds, small mammals, and insects, which also find nourishment in its fruits, leaves, and bark. Its wood is fashioned into furniture and other useful items, and its fruits or nuts might be shipped thousands of miles and end up in our grocery store. The tree emerges, not in isolated beauty, but in a many-leveled texture of relationships.

Man-made objects can be treated similarly. A Chinese vase has connections with the clay from the earth, with the universally used wheel, on which it was shaped, with the culture in which the artist lived, and with his personal interpretation.

The people we contact everyday have within them the attitudes and values of their families and cultural backgrounds, the influence of their education, the important people in their lives, and ideas that they have internalized from many sources. We are not facing an individual with strict boundaries but a person who is an open system and who channels many streams, as we ourselves do.

If we practice mental exercises such as these, we can train our minds to look for connections and see the wide background and milieu of people and things. We may come to realize, as H.P.B. says, that " . . . no manifested thing can be thought of except as part of a whole." We begin to break the deeply ingrained habit of dividing reality into separate compartments and of perceiving the world in separate units.

Such exercises are techniques we can use to experience the world more holistically, to realize that our being is enmeshed in endless ways with others and with our environment. We may find many other ways to chip away at our sense of isolation and to glimpse ourselves in that great unity described by Hippocrates when he said: "There is one common flow, one common breathing: all things are in sympathy."

4

The Transcendent Source

The universe produced from the one undivided Atman by the on-rolling process of manifestation is a
unified system, a mighty organism in which the inmost nucleus and pervading Spirit and Self is the one
abiding Being . . . every part, every particle in it is
ensouled, inspirited, by the All-aware All-feeling
Being that is Atman.

J.C. Chatterji

*T*heosophy points to a unity deeper than that of interrela-
tionships between manifest wholes. The teaching rests
on the fundamental concept of an overarching oneness in the
invisible, transcendental realm. Everything that exists at any
level of being springs from this numinous source, the creative
fount behind manifestation. Though itself completely nonmaterial, it gives rise to all degrees of materiality. As clouds
form from invisible water vapor, so all things condense from
this invisible background. Or according to the *Mandukya
Upanishad*, "As a spider throws out and retracts its
web . . . so the Universe is derived from the undecaying
one." The One "becomes the universe woven out of its own
essence," in H.P.B.'s words.

Mystical experience confirms the esoteric teaching that, in
spite of the seeming divisions in the foreground, this realm
remains whole and undivided. Its wholeness is reflected in the
interconnections among all manifested things perceived in

holism. The coordination of wholes visible everywhere in nature—the intricate web of connections—is the outworking in the world of the basic unity from which it arises.

The noumenal, nonmaterial Source of all remains forever one and undivided, while the interconnections and wholeness perceived in the world reflect this background oneness. Prem and Ashish refer to these as two directions in which the world is linked into a unity—the vertical and the horizontal, as expressed in the ancient symbol of the cross. The vertical represents transcendence, the oneness between the world and its transcendental Source. The horizontal stands for the One permeating the many, and the interlinking of all phenomena in the manifest world.[1]

We have seen that some scientists have come to acknowledge holism and the interconnectedness of phenomena in the world. Presently we shall see how the noumenal background Reality is also recognized in modern physics.

The Rootless Root

Speaking of this transcendent Source, H.P.B. says, " . . . there is One Absolute Reality which antecedes all manifested, conditioned Being. This Infinite and Eternal cause . . . is the Rootless Root of 'all that was, or ever shall be.' "[2] Though this Reality "transcends the power of human conception and could only be dwarfed by any human expression of similitude," she uses powerful words which help us glimpse something of its awesome nature. She describes it as "an Omnipresent, Eternal, Boundless and Immutable Principle."[3] Each of these terms can serve as a subject for meditation in which we try to stretch our minds to realize more deeply what the One Reality might be.

According to theosophical teaching, this transcendental Source is not identical with nor exhausted by creation; only a portion of the All becomes involved in the process of manifestation. It might be compared to a dancer who emodies certain ideas and feelings in a dance. That dance is an authentic expression of the dancer's potential, which is revealed in the movements. Still, there remain vast areas not enacted in this performance, any number of ideas, feelings, movements, styles, roles the dancer is capable of. Any one dance is only a partial manifestion of the potential of the dancer. Perhaps Krishna, representing the One, meant something like this when he said in the *Bhagavad Gita*, "Having pervaded this whole universe with one fragment of Myself, I remain."

According to esoteric philosophy, the One is never apart from the process of manifesting seemingly separate beings. Rather, the world is an essential aspect of the all-containing oneness, an integral part of the Whole. The creative background Reality does not stand outside the universe that emerges from it, but is present in every part, in every transient phenomenon, each fragment depending on the One for its existence. All nature is the outcome and the reflection of the One, which is its ground, and lies embedded in that Oneness from which it can never be really separate.

Thus the world of manifestation in all its variety reveals That from which it arises: "The root of every atom individually and every form collectively is . . . the One Reality."[4] And again:

> The Marvels of the One Spirit of Truth, the ever-concealed and inaccessible Deity, can be unravelled and assimilated only through its manifestation . . . . While the One and Universal cause has to remain forever *in abscondito*, its manyfold action may be traced through the effects in Nature.[5]

While we can never fully know the unreachable Divine Source in its purity, we can approach it in its numberless manifestations, as it "thrills throughout every atom and infinitesimal point of the whole Kosmos."[6] H.P.B. refers to the "One Universal Element which is infinite, unborn, undying" yet appears everywhere in nature in endless guises that are really "so many various differentiated aspects and transformations of that One."[7] This background Reality has the marvelous, paradoxical quality of being simultaneously the One and the many, even though the manifested "many" expresses only a small portion of the infinite potential of the One. Jacob Boehme expressed this idea when he said that nature bears the *Signatura Rerum,* the seal or signature of the eternal within things. Jesus said, "Raise the stone and thou shalt find me, cleave the wood and I am there" (Gospel of Thomas). The concept of the Divine in nature is expressed beautifully from the Eastern point of view by J. C. Chatterji: " . . . the universe, with everything in it, is only an outward flow and a crystallized form of the unceasingly upwelling Joy of Brahman."[8]

If we could learn to pierce anything deeply enough with a quiet mind, to go beyond its appearance to its essence, we might at least momentarily catch a ray of the divine light within it. In its depths the life in all that exists *is* the One Life. If we can sense this life in one person or natural object, we can sense that it also exists in everyone and in all nature. We might rediscover the mystical insight that at a deep level the one creative life pervades all with deep joy and peace.

Physics and Mysticism

Science has come upon a nonmaterial background Reality through more objective methods. It is astonishing that physics, the "hardest," most rigorous of sciences, has penetrated matter as we ordinarily know it and come out in a numinous, nonmaterial world similar to that described by H.P.B. The poetic, mystical insight of antiquity seems at the opposite pole from modern physics with its particle accelerators, bubble chambers, and precise mathematical formulations. Yet the two views are merging. Fritjof Capra, drawing parallels between modern physics and the mystics's view of reality, a view which is very much in keeping with theosophy, says:

> The mystic is looking at the everyday, ordinary reality in a non-ordinary mode of perception, and perceives this reality, somehow, in its very essence or in a more fundamental way, a deeper way. The patterns and principles of organization that emerge from that experience are very similar to the patterns and principles of organization we observe in physics when we go to very small dimensions.[9]

This is a complete reversal of the position of classical physics, based on the mechanistic, materialistic views of Descartes, Galileo, and Newton. Under the domination of the mechanistic position, science was restricted to studying only properties of material bodies which could be quantified and measured. All aspects of complex phenomena, including living creatures, were thought to be best understood by reducing them to their constituent parts and studying the parts.

Operating from this position, 19th- and early 20th-century physicists probed the atom as the basic, smallest fragment of the material world and searched for tiny, isolable building blocks with mass, which comprise all material things. This search led them into an entirely unexpected realm as materiality dissolved before their gaze.

Physicists came to view atoms, not as material bits of mass, but as energy with electrical charges. For a long time, electrons, protons, and neutrons were thought to be the absolutely unchangeable and indivisible constituents of matter. But the particles slipped away from the grasp like sand through the fingers when the particles were discovered to have a wave-like aspect, sometimes appearing only as waves and not as particles at all. The nucleus, which contains essentially all of the mass of the atom, under probing experimentation dissolved into innumerable fleeting particles.

Modern nuclear physics with its particle accelerators, which hurl particles around tracks at nearly the speed of light, and bubble chambers, which make it possible to photograph the path of particles moving in liquid helium, has discovered hundreds of subatomic particles, most extremely short-lived. These, Merlin-like, swiftly decay into other particles, and it has been found that any type of subatomic particle can be transformed into any other type. The word *particle* takes on a new meaning. It is not a distinct, indestructible unit with a consistent identity but a dynamic pattern with a certain amount of energy that can be modified into other particles. According to some physicists, subatomic particles have no meaning as isolated entities.

These extremely dynamic packets of energy form relatively stable atomic and molecular structures which look like substance built up into things. But at the subatomic level there is nothing substantial. The reality behind the physical world is a

Pierre Maluc's painting Apex *suggests the dynamic pattern of energy that underlies the physical world.*

ceaseless flow of energy. At the subatomic level the world would appear as darts of light, bright patches emerging from darkness, a rhythmic dance of small scintillations.[10] Physics has shown us that the world of the senses is at base a flux of energy; our senses show us only phantasmagoria resting on a quite different foundation. This view upholds the age-old philosophical and religious contention that sense experience is unreliable, misleading, a maya or illusion that does not match reality. In Capra's view the basis of the physical world turns out to be unitive, a pattern of energy, not a collection of discrete and separated things.*

The insubstantiality of the subatomic level found in nuclear physics might leave us feeling insecure in an unstable flux. However, physics shows us something stable and fundamental underlying this perpetual motion. This is the field, a non-material constant behind the transient physical world. Field theory arose in physics to explain action at a distance. The electromagnetic field is well known through its effect on magnets and in various electrical phenomena, and other fields such as the gravitational are also familiar. Contemporary physicists describe the interactions between subatomic particles in terms of fields by combining ideas from classical field theory with quantum theory (which deals with packets of energy at the subatomic level). Particles are seen as local and changing conditions in the underlying, continuous field, which is fundamental. Capra states that "the quantum field is seen as the fundamental physical entity: a continuous medium which is present everywhere in space." In this regard Einstein says:

> We may therefore regard matter as being constituted by the regions of space in which the field is extremely intense . . . .

---

*The majority of mainstream physicists subscribe to the quark model, which hypothesizes that the many subatomic particles that have been discovered are composed of more fundamental units, quarks. A few varieties of quarks are believed to exist. There is some evidence for this theory, but it is not yet definitely substantiated. The quark model contrasts with the "bootstrap theory" presented here, which emphasizes interactions among particles rather than the question of the composition of the particles themselves.

> There is no place in this new kind of physics for both the field
> and matter, for the field is the only reality.[11]

Thus particles are but fleeting conditions in the abiding field,
concentrations of energy which emerge from the field and
dissolve back. They have been found to appear out of
"nothing." In other words, the field generates matter, brings it
into being from itself, and draws it back into "nothing." According to Capra, "the field [or the Void] is not a state of mere
nothingness but contains the potentiality for all forms of the
particle world. These forms, in turn, are not independent
physical entities but merely transient manifestations of the
underlying Void."[12] In *The Voice of the Silence* H.P.B. speaks
of "the voidness of the seeming full, the fullness of the seeming void."

In this context of field theory as in nuclear physics, the col-
orful, varied world we perceive, which seems so real and solid
and immediate, becomes a passing manifestation of an underlying nonmaterial continuum, the field. Science now confirms
the insubstantiality and transiency of the world, which
religions have long upheld. The seemingly solid, separate
things we experience through our senses are not solid or
separate at base but emerge from the same unitary background, which is the primary reality.

For ages theosophy and Eastern philosophy have held a
view like this. The new knowledge from physics supports and
corroborates an ancient insight. It gives an added dimension
to our understanding of the background reality, a precise for-
mulation to an age-old intuition. Although it does not encompass all the dimensions of reality, modern physics throws new
light on our understanding of the transcendental Source.

F. L. Kunz, a pioneer in promoting a unitary view based on
science, saw the relation between Eastern philosophy and
modern physics many years ago. He saw the fundamental
change in world view necessitated by the concept of fields,
and its parallels with theosophical and Eastern philosophy. In
his expanded view of fields he regarded the background field
as affecting more than just the world of physics. He saw it as
the durable, real source of all the ephemeral foreground

phenomena of the world, which are its partial expression: " . . . the sensed material cosmos, as such, and man as a creature evolved in it, occur in a wholly nonmaterial reality which is unchanged by the comings and goings of such evolving systems."[13] The world we see is derived from this causal domain, which directs and governs the natural world, and the laws of nature result from its characteristics and structure. Things in the foreground are finite, localized conditions of the field which is infinite, universal, and continuous throughout space.

This perspective of fields, which predates the contemporary interest in wholeness, leads to a unitive worldview which includes an ethics and way of life which takes all life into consideration. Kunz says:

> It is necessary for us all to begin to think in terms of universals—a universe—unlocalized, not a universe that consists of sensed objects as if they are collectively the whole. The whole *is*, in its own right, and it is nonmaterial (but real), continuous, characterizable. *Au fond*, it determines what things can and cannot be.[14]

He equated this background reality to the Indian view of Brahman and the theosophical Absolute or One Reality. More recently Capra, too, has pointed out parallels in field theory to Eastern concepts of a divine ground from which the world derives.

> The Brahman of the Hindus, the Dharmakaya of the Buddhists, and the Tao of the Taoists, can be seen perhaps, as the ultimate unified field from which spring not only the phenomena studied in physics, but all other phenomena as well.[15]

The Holographic Model

In recent times another model has emerged from science that is also striking in its similarity to Eastern and esoteric philosophy. David Bohm, a theoretical physicist and former associate of Einstein, bases this model on the principles of holography. He pictures reality as an unbroken whole in which every fragment—every cell, atom, small chunk of matter—contains the entire universe, "a world in a grain of sand," as Blake put it.

Holography is a method of lensless photography. Its most unusual feature is that the entire image of an object is contained in every fragment of the plate. In Bohm's model of the universe, the holographic image or picture is analogous to the space-time world of the senses, the realm of separate objects. But rather than being the primary reality, this image is the outcome of the moving pattern of light bouncing off the object photographed. The image we see would be what Bohm calls the "explicit order" or "unfolded order," the manifestation in time and space of a reality from another, deeper dimension. Although captured on the photographic plate, the pattern of light actually exists only as waves and frequencies. This pattern is the "implicate" or "enfolded" order from which the image derives.

Objects and events in nature are carried not only by light but by electron beams, sound, and innumerable other ways. The *holomovement* is Bohm's name for the totality of all these carriers of the implicate order. This is the unbroken, flowing, ever-changing movement of all frequencies: light, sound, electron beams, all fields, both known and yet to be discovered.

Television provides an analogy. The visual image from the camera at the studio must be translated into radio waves which transmit it to our homes. The pattern in radio waves by no means has a one-to-one correspondence with the visual image. Yet the image is enfolded or implicated in the radio waves. Our television sets then unfold or explicate the order of the image, again making it visible or manifest.

In this holographic model again we see the world we know as emerging from a nonmaterial background, in this case a numinous flowing world of energy and complex frequencies which carries patterns for everything which manifests from it.

The holomovement in the background is much vaster than what is unfolded or manifest in the world. As Bohm says, " . . . this implicate order implies a reality immensely beyond what we call matter. Matter itself is merely a ripple in this background . . . and the ocean of energy is not primarily in space and time at all."[16] As Krishna puts it in the *Gita*, "Having pervaded this whole universe with one fragment of myself, I remain."

While Bohm was developing his theory, Karl Pribram, a brain researcher at Stanford, was also working on a holographic model. An impressive body of research from many laboratories has shown that the brain somehow analyzes frequencies in time and space, which it translates into seeing, hearing, touching, etc. The brain, like a hologram, distributes this information through the whole of itself, so that each fragment is encoded to reproduce the information of the whole. Thus Pribram came to see the brain's "deep structure" as holographic: it employs a holographic process to abstract from a holographic domain. After Pribram and Bohm had each developed his own theory independently, they discovered each other's work and began to collaborate. The holographic model they developed emphasizes the unity and wholeness of reality, which is the basic tenet of theosophical teachings and of Eastern philosophy.

Thus in our times we see the historical moment in which physics corroborates the existence of a nonmaterial reality from which the physical world arises. Far-sighted physicists have even glimpsed the magnitude of this background reality, which theosophy sees as extending far beyond the scope of physics to encompass all realms of nature. A consideration of true universals in nature, such as space, time, and motion, can lead us to a glimpse of the all-pervasive character of this unitive Source.

5

The Divinity of Space

> There is no difference between the Christian
> Apostle's "In Him we live and move and have our be-
> ing" (*Acts* xvii, 28) and the Hindu Rishi's "The
> Universe lives in, proceeds from, and will return to
> Brahman" . . . . The God of the Apostle-Initiate and
> of the Rishi being both the Unseen and the visible
> SPACE.
>
> *The Secret Doctrine*

Motion, space, and time are among the few true universals which cross all boundaries and touch all existence.
Mystics and scientists have found dimensions of these three
realities that are dramatically different from the way in which
we ordinarily experience them, so all-encompassing that they
take on a divine aspect.

At first glance space, time, and motion seem ordinary
aspects of our mundane world. They are so pervasive, so constant and familiar that we do not even notice them. Yet on
reflection we must acknowledge that nothing exists which is
not in motion—perceptible as a cat springing or imperceptible
as a mountain slowly eroding, the dance of atoms, or the orbiting planets. Space, too, is everywhere—in the box-like
areas of our rooms, in the immensity of galactic distances, in
the ultramicroscopic areas of subatomic particles. Time is an
intrinsic part of all existence, which we experience as the
pressure of the moment or the passing of our days and years,

as the age of our universe from its beginning, or the instantaneous nanoseconds of subatomic particles.

Each of these three aspects of reality can be seen in many guises, so many, in fact, that they may hardly seem related. We know a great deal about each of them from many points of view. But whatever we know and experience of motion, space, and time is only the outer appearance of the deeper mystery behind these three, for theosophy teaches that they are attributes of the nonmaterial Reality, the One. In *The Secret Doctrine* H.P.B. proclaims that they are three aspects of the Absolute, the primeval Source of all. In the *Mahatma Letters*, written by H.P.B.'s teachers, these three are depicted as themselves being the Reality which generates everything: " . . . all phenomena proceed from infinite space, duration and motion."[1] In their infinite and limitless guise, motion, space, and time are identical with that background which gives rise to all the phenomena in the foreground of our knowledge and experience. They are universal, eternal, ever-present, divine.

We will look at each of these three facets of Reality as it appears to us in our experience and also as it is perceived in modern thought. In this way we will try to glimpse the metaphysical Reality that underlies the motion, space, and time that we know in the world, and see if it is possible in some measure to experience their sublime aspect.

The Many Guises of Space

Eastern philosophy and theosophy posit Ultimate Space which, as it were, casts its shadow to form our world of time and space. The many varieties of space that we experience are derived from this Universal Space and reflect it. In *The Secret Doctrine* it is symbolized as Dark Space, not the bright space of the manifested world, but the mysterious depths from which the latter arises. This dark matrix has been compared to our unconscious mind, from which emerges the light of our waking consciousness.[2] In this undifferentiated, boundless Space there are no dimensions, no directions, no inside and outside, no here and there. It is the depth and breadth from

which directions of space arise, the dimensionless continuum from which spatial dimensions emerge. Thus Space in the metaphysical sense used by H.P.B. is the "one eternal thing" that "was and ever will be."

We experience many expressions of this background of Universal Space. In recent decades we have been thrilled by the exploration of outer space—men walking on the moon, probes penetrating distant planets, shuttles orbiting the earth. Space themes in movies, fiction, even advertisements both stimulate and reflect this interest. Pictures of the night sky with countless galaxies or of the earth as seen from the moon have etched themselves into our subconscious mind so that the perspective of outer space begins to color all our thinking. We also hear of stars thousands of times larger than our sun, galaxies hundreds of thousands of light years across, endless space that curves on itself and is expanding at an unimaginable rate, like the outside of a cosmic balloon being blown up. As we learn more and more of outer space, it becomes even more mysterious and intriguing.

In addition to the call of outer space, the humble space all around us conceals a mystery for us to explore. Space continually impinges on our consciousness in subliminal ways, and its character seems to change as we experience it from different standpoints. The confinement we feel in an elevator contrasts sharply with the freedom we experience in the country or an open field; the restrictions of a valley affect us quite differently from the openness of a mountain top. Some people have become seriously ill from their fear of heights or of tightly confined spaces.

We usually think of space as an emptiness which holds discrete things—chairs, houses, cities. We also experience it as the medium through which things move; we continually pass through it as we walk, ride, fly. As distance between locations, it is spread out and has directions. Maps are based on this directional property of space. But distance and direction are unimportant for the space within things. Inner emptiness is everywhere and can be the essential feature—space inside a pitcher, inside a shoe, inside our stomach or lungs.

Space to the painter, artist, or landscape architect means a background for composition, a boundary in which to place elements in artistic balance. To the scientist, concepts of space are concealed in sophisticated mathematical formulae. Space is flexible, changeable, has a protean ability to appear in many guises.

Spatial Perspectives

Our usual way of perceiving space through three-dimensional perspective is deceiving. We are each in the center of a circle from which increasing distance makes things appear smaller and smaller. We are the reference point for distance; we see space receding from us. We are the center of our universe. This reinforces our ingrained egocentricity which leads to a sense of isolation. But photos of lunar or stellar spaces give quite a different perspective, showing our relative place in an immensity where it is hard to maintain exaggerated self-concern. Here, too, the boundaries we experience in space—our skin, our home, our city, state, nation, even continent—become unimportant in the vastness. The unthinkable distance between stars and between galaxies also shows us the relative proportion of space to matter in the universe, space being far more extensive than the matter within it.

When we go to the very small, we also find space preponderant. We recall that even in solid, rigid materials such as granite, there is space between the molecules. An atom is mostly empty space. If the nucleus were magnified to the size of a grape seed, the electrons would circle the Astrodome. If the nucleus were magnified to the size of a pea, the nearest nucleus would be about 0.6 mile away. There are even spaces in the seemingly tightly packed nucleus. If a sphere with circumference the size of a period on this page were made of touching nuclei, the sphere would weigh more than a million tons. Astronomers estimate that all the matter of the earth collapsed into a black hole of nuclei packed together would occupy about one cubic inch. The illusively solid world is mostly empty space.

Einstein gave us a view quite different from the naive concept of things occupying empty, static space. Einstein's space is not an empty box that stays the same regardless of its contents. There is no absolute space, no inert background medium that remains static and unchanged. He showed us space as dynamic, its shape changed by what is in it and that shape in turn affecting what goes on. In his General Theory of Relativity he held that large amounts of matter perceptibly warp space. It becomes curved around massive bodies like the sun, as the grid on a net is deformed when hit by a volleyball. This curvature is what makes planets and satellites move in circular orbits. Van Gogh unconsciously anticipated this idea when he painted skies with heavy curvatures surrounding the sun or stars. In the Einsteinian universe, matter structures space and space determines the movement of matter. Space is an active, structuring medium with dramatic features, and it cannot be separated from matter.

Einstein expanded our view even further to show how space and time are interwoven into a four-dimensional space-time continuum, thus adding another dimension to the world. John Wheeler, who has been referred to as "the grand old man of theoretical physics," went further and concluded that space has an infinite number of dimensions. Contemplating physics, he felt there must be a "superspace," beyond the four-dimensional realm, endowed with an infinite number of dimensions. "The stage on which the space of the universe moves is certainly not space itself . . . . The arena must be a larger object: superspace."[3]

Universal Space

Theosophy teaches that even this expanded space of Einstein or Wheeler is only the outer expression of the Universal Space of metaphysics. Writing before Einstein's time, H.P.B. implied that space has more than four dimensions when she referred to it as "seven-skinned," and elsewhere as without dimensions. Inspired by *The Secret Doctrine*, Prem and Ashish wrote of this limitless space: " . . . the four-dimensional 'curved' space-time of experience is a limited enclosure within the utterly undimensioned and atemporal space of the Matrix . . ."[4]

This abstract Space, which symbolizes the Absolute One, is immutable. All the violent explosions of stars being born and dying, of life arising and declining, of human passion, tragedy, and ecstasy do not in any way affect this changeless background. Unlike Einstein's space, Universal Space is "immovable in its abstraction and uninfluenced by either the presence or absence in it of an objective universe."[5] It is timeless. Epochs of history, individual lives, planets, stars, galaxies come and go, while Absolute Abstract Space endures forever. It is the "limitless void" that contains all that is, whether manifest or not. In this sense it is boundless, eternal emptiness.

However, Universal Space is not only the container: it is the generator of all manifestation. We have seen that particles can emerge from a background field. Theosophy teaches that all manifestation emerges from seemingly empty Space, as foam from water, as the *Upanishads* have it. Uncountable universes come and go without exhausting its infinite potential. This Space is also conditioned fullness, a Plenum, in that in it lies the potential for everything that is, was, or will be. H.P.B. equated Space with the "Absolute All." In this sense it can be identified with undifferentiated Consciousness, as will be discussed in Chapter 10, on polarity. In the theosophical conception, Space—the divine Source of all being—stands eternally behind the coming and going of worlds, the stable background upholding all that is transient. It is that noumenal Reality from which all arises and into which all eventually withdraws. Joseph Campbell, an authority on mythology, could have been referring to the theosophical concept of Space when he wrote:

> Briefly formulated, the universal doctrine teaches that all the visible structures of the world—all things and being— are the effects of a ubiquitous power out of which they rise, which supports and fills them during the period of their manifestation, and back into which they must ultimately dissolve.[6]

In spite of the many faces that space shows us, there are not several distinct spaces. All of our experience is pervaded by the dimension of Universal Space, what the Tibetan teacher Tarthang calls Great Space. The ordinary mundane space we experience is an expression of that vast cosmic principle which lies at its heart. We are not usually aware of this infinity because our focal setting is trained on a smaller perspective, but we can learn to widen our view.

Meditation can stretch and enlarge our mind so that in some sense Great Space becomes a reality to us. The sky, a wide expanse of emptiness, is a natural symbol for Space.

Gazing at the sky on a clear night, we sense something of the boundlessness and infinity of endless Space. The visible expanse of sky before us tells of something beyond, even more vast—an endless continuum that stretches forever, far beyond any visible galaxies.

It is possible by contemplating Space in meditation to recapture this sense of expansion. In imagination we can again reach out and lose ourselves in that immensity. If we then turn to the familiar spaces around us—bounded in our buildings, rooms, streets, yards—we can realize that though these are broken up and cut into pieces, they are permeated by the vastness of Great Space. Though they appear confined, they are in no way separate from that unbroken, frontierless continuum.

We can also train ourselves no longer to look only at the hard outlines of things that make them stand out as discrete. We can think of the spaces within things, their emptiness and hollows, the spaces between their particles, which are also part of Space. Then the distinct separation between things and their background dissolves and Space is seen to penetrate everywhere and through all that exists. In ways like this we can cultivate consciousness of Space and learn to see it around us and within us all the time. Then Great Space is no longer an abstraction removed from our lives but becomes a reality that embraces and upholds us every moment of our lives.

6

The Cosmic Heartbeat

> The absolute attribute (of the One Life), which is
> Itself eternal, ceaseless Motion, is called in esoteric
> parlance the 'Great Breath,' which is the perpetual
> motion of the universe, in the sense of limitless ever-
> present Space. That which is motionless cannot be
> Divine. But then there is nothing in fact and reality
> absolutely motionless within the universal soul.
>
> *The Secret Doctrine*

Motion is inescapable. Wherever we look, at whatever level of being, we can find nothing still or at rest. In the natural world the imperceptible growth of trees and the gradual wearing away of rocks are just as surely motion as the shiver of poplar leaves in the wind, the falling of snow, or the clapping of children's hands. Our own inner processes, too, flow perpetually. The heart pumps blood endlessly to our cells, which are in constant activity as they absorb nutrients, expel wastes, divide and reproduce themselves. The materials of all our tissues are constantly changing, some with spectacular rates of growth and renewal. Our thoughts and feelings, too, are constantly moving and changing, as we become vividly aware when we try to still the mind in meditation.

The astronomical world is even more dramatic in its ceaseless, often violent activity. Even as our planet races around the sun and the sun shifts around our galaxy, all

Children embody the perpetual motion of the universe.

astronomical bodies are hurtling through space at incredible speeds. Stars, including our own sun, continually release enormous explosions of atomic energy from the nucleus of their atoms. X-ray galaxies, so hot that they dissolve atomic nuclei, emit high energy radiation, some releasing a billion times more energy than does our sun. Whether or not we perceive it, the world around us and we ourselves are in a state of constant motion, violent or subdued, that will continue forever.

For thousands of years the philosophy of India has known that motion is of the essence of existence. Speaking from this point of view, the Indian scholar J. C. Chatterji said: "There is nothing absolutely stable, nothing permanently abiding, in the whole of the objective universe, which is but a system of ceaseless 'goings on' . . . with everything in it continually moving and changing . . ."[1]

Continuous change is also a fundamental axiom of the *Secret Doctrine.* H.P.B. teaches that "motion is eternal," that there is ceaseless motion throughout the boundless reaches of infinitude. She makes a distinction—and at the same time a connection—between abstract Motion as an eternal principle and the motions we know in nature. The "metaphysical One Absolute Be-ness" or Reality is symbolized in two ways: absolute abstract Space and absolute abstract Motion, referred to as the Great Breath. Abstract Motion is transcendent, an aspect of the One, no different from the transcendent Source behind all that is. "Intra-cosmic motion," which is eternal and ceaseless, is contrasted with "cosmic motion . . . that which is subject to perception [and therefore] is finite and periodical. As an eternal abstraction [Motion] is Ever-Present; as a manifestation it is finite."[2] As with space, this noumenal counterpart of motion is the Source of all the movements that we experience and science investigates. Thus theosophy perceives the varieties of motion in nature as expressions and variations of a noumenal rhythm. The ceaseless changes of the world around us and within us derive their impetus from the eternal cosmic heartbeat of the Transcendent Source.

Little can be said of the noumenal Great Breath, "that which is and yet is not . . . which we can only speak of as absolute existence, but cannot picture to our imagination as any form of existence that we can distinguish."[3] Noumenal Reality is beyond the reach of human thought. However, both science and theosophy have much to say about the perpetual motion in the universe, and they are in agreement on some essential points.

Motion: Physical and Metaphysical

Speaking of movements in the familiar material world, H.P.B. states that "it is a fundamental law of Occultism that there is no rest or cessation of motion in Nature."[4] Speaking from the viewpoint of modern physics, Fritjof Capra states that "matter is never quiescent but always in a state of motion."[5] Physics has shown that matter itself is inconceivable without motion. Anticipating this view, though written at the end of the 19th century in an age in which matter was considered dead and inert and needed force to set it in motion, *The Mahatma Letters* states: "No atom is ever in an absolute state of rest."[6] Einstein, too, recognized that we live in a dynamic universe in which everything is in perpetual motion. The author Serviss describes Einstein's views:

> . . . a universe in which everything had a tendency to stop its own motion would soon become a dead universe, destitute of any life or activity whatever. But scientific investigations show that in infinitely little, as well as infinitely great things, *all is motion* . . . we find *nothing at rest.*
>
> This being so, says Einstein in effect, motion must be regarded as the natural, as well as the actual condition of matter, a state of things that needs no explanation from us, for it arises out of the very constitution of the universe. It is the very essence of existence.[7]

Theosophy agrees with physics that motion is not imposed by any outer force, as was supposed in Newtonian physics, but is a characteristic of matter itself. While Capra holds that "the forces causing the motion are not outside the object but are an intrinsic property of matter,"[8] *The Mahatma Letters* claims that "motion is a manner of existence that flows necessarily out of the essence of matter."[9] Physics and theosophy agree that motion is built into the very foundation of the universe, in the atoms that are its basis. There can be no material world without motion.

From the viewpoint of theosophical metaphysics, motion is not only an essential characteristic of all material things but is also the basis for the many forms of energy in the world. Motion may be conceived as the primal source from which arise any number of different forms of energy, as white light is the source of the colors of the rainbow. *The Mahatma Letters* states the theosophical view of the relation between motion and the various kinds of energy:

> . . . since motion is all-pervading and absolute rest inconceivable, under whatever form of *mask* motion may appear, whether as light, heat, magnetism, chemical affinity or electricity—all these must be but phases of One and the same universal omnipotent Force [which] we simply call the "One Life," the "One Law" and the "One Element."[10]

The search in modern physics for a unified field which binds together gravity, all electro-magnetic forces, and nuclear energy suggests that scientists since Einstein give credence to this concept of a unified Force as posited in esoteric philosophy.

As already discussed, it is not only the world of atoms and subatomic particles that is in constant motion. Objects, lives, and beings at every level are always moving, changing. Capra says, "The cosmos is seen as one reality, forever in motion . . . ."[11] *The Mahatma Letters* hints at the far-reaching effects of motion in the formation of the world as we know it: "It is motion with its resulting conflict, neutralization, equilibration, correlation to which is due the infinite variety which prevails."[12]

Rhythm and the Great Breath

H.P.B. depicts the innumerable cycles throughout nature as resting on the pulsing, rhythmic motion behind all (chapter 12). Her image for the eternal movement underlying cycles is the Great Breath, "the Breath of the One Existence," while motion "is its equivalent in the material plane."[13] In nature the rhythms and cycles are periodical; they come and go, but the noumenal "Motion is eternal in the unmanifested."[14] Thus a picture emerges of a steady, eternal pulsing in the non-material background to which resonate a myriad of rhythms and pulses in the world—"the eternal pulse, the archetype of all the rhythms in the universe."[15]

We see reflections of this universal pulse in such earthly rhythms as that of the slime mold which grows in forests. The protoplasm of this simple form of life is not confined in cells but flows freely in rhythmic pulses, back and forth, over and over, in a regular beat. Another such reflection of the universal heartbeat appears in the development of an embryo. Films show a beating in the chest area of an embryonic chick well before the heart has formed. All the breathing, the pulses, the rhythms and movements of the natural world on earth or in astronomical spaces are variations of the one universal pulse, which gives rise to them. Thus, theosophical thought probes universal motion to its depths in noumenal Reality, which is not mechanical and dead but rather the One Life, pulsing continuously throughout all time and space.

The motion reflected from this inner cosmic pulse can vary in intensity at different times as universes and cycles go through their various phases. As Prem and Ashish put it:

> Forever and forever, that Life pulses within the heart of all that is. Its ageless, tireless rhythm is sometimes strong and sometimes faint as the cycles go through their appointed course, but it never ceases altogether.[16]

Thus, according to theosophy, universes come and go, but the pulsing movement of the One is never stilled, even during intervals in which nothing is manifest and there are no things, no material universe, only the one homogeneous Life in darkness and silence. The Stanzas of Dzyan in *The Secret Doctrine* describe a precosmic stage when "Life pulsated unconscious in Universal Space." It is almost impossible for us to imagine movement and rhythm in a state of total quiescence with nothing to move. Yet the eternal breath continues. Chatterji compares this state to "a waveless flow, as there may be in an ocean." When the multifarious universes emerge, the flow continues, but it erupts into currents, "giving rise to all kinds of eddies, ripples, and waves, which are diversified objects."[17]

The temple music of Tibet exemplifies this relation between one rhythm and many. The long trumpet is blown continuously, its deep tone sounding an uninterrupted *Om*. Strains from various instruments rise above this and move in different melodies, rhythms, and configurations of sound, but eventually die back into the undying *Om*.

Crosscurrents also exist in us, but seldom harmonized as in music. Much of the time we may feel pulled apart, jangled, scattered, as though several conflicting rhythms were churning inside us as in turbulent waters. At other times, particularly if we meditate, the turbulence subsides and the waters of our psyche become calm. Such stillness can come from the yoga practice of being aware of our breathing, or listening to inner rhythms like the heartbeat, or chanting the *Om*. In moments of intense stillness when the breath has become deep and slow and the sound of the Om has died away, some meditators report sensing a slow, steady, inner beat, not any bodily rhythm, but a silent pulsing from a deeper level of consciousness. Like the downbeat that unifies the instruments of the orchestra, this basic beat can harmonize all the levels of our being into a synchronous flow. Such an experience in meditation can help us to understand the cosmic process in which a single fundamental rhythm beats below and gives rise to the many diverse rhythms in the world.

7

Time and Timelessness

Kronos stands for endless, and hence immovable
Duration, without beginning, without end, beyond
divided Time and beyond Space.
The Secret Doctrine

*I*n his *Confessions*, St. Augustine said that he knew what
time was when no one inquired, but did not know when he
was asked to explain it. If someone asks us, What is time? we,
too, may feel bewildered. We have intimate knowledge of
time as calendar time, time for dinner or an appointment,
how long it takes to write a letter or get to work. We know
time as waltz time, time out, the years of our lives, the ages of
history. We have heard of the immensity of light years in
astronomy and the fleeting nanoseconds in nuclear physics.
Our experience of time passing is familiar and pervasive, yet
we seldom stop to consider what time really is. Past, present,
and future are built into our conception of the world; we
assume that they describe time. But we are apt to take these at
face value without probing their true nature.

H.P.B. says that "our ideas . . . on duration and time are
all derived from our sensations according to the law of

association, inextricably bound up with the relativity of human knowledge."[1] This, she feels, is inadequate to express the nuances and subtleties of time as presented in esoteric philosophy. Past, present, and future are gross categories produced by our minds by which we experience events in succession, "the panoramic succession of our states of consciousness."[2] These three are divided from one another, "compound" only in relation to the phenomenal plane, but in the realm of noumena have no . . . validity."[3] In the transcendent noumenal world, time in the sense of our sequential experiences does not exist. There is no movement from past to present or into the future, for "the Past Time is the Present Time, as also the Future, which, though it has not yet come into existence, still is."[4]

Such an idea of all events existing simultaneously in a timeless state may be incomprehensible to our finite minds. We will consider the concept later and make H.P.B.'s teaching more explicit, as well as exploring its relation to modern physics. For now, it is enough to realize that time, like space and motion, has roots in the noumenon where its guise is very different from its appearance in our familiar world. H.P.B. equates time with space and both with the nonmaterial Reality that underlies all being. "Space and Time are one. Space and Time are nameless, for they are the uncognizable THAT."[5] Nameless though the source of time may be, she nevertheless gives it a name—Duration.

H.P.B. conceives time in the manifested world differently from the linear, one-way flow produced by our minds. She repeatedly speaks of cycles, of the periodic coming and going of universes and beings that go through stages of development, then return to the starting point, only to repeat the pattern, as can be illustrated by flowering and seed-making. This cyclic view, typical of Eastern philosophy, appears again and again in *The Secret Doctrine*, which views manifestation at all levels as periodic, recurring, rhythmic outflow and return (chapter 12). All nature—from universes and galaxies to fireflies and cells—works on this principle, and it is also the pattern for human growth and development.

Time: Linear and Cyclic

However, our ordinary experience of time contrasts with the all-encompassing timelessness of Duration as well as with the cyclic view. For us time seems like a river that flows out of the past into the future. Events seem to occur in an unending succession of moments which move past us. The immediate present seems to have appeared out of the past and to be vanishing into the future, always in the same direction—forward. Past-present-future are further divided into discrete intervals, packets of time which differentiate the uniform, linear flow and make it more manageable. We measure these segments with clocks and calendars and regulate our lives and activities accordingly. We are dominated by the clock more than we realize. We fragment ourselves into units of measured time.

Subconsciously we feel the river of time must flow at a constant rate. This concept, based on Newton's view of the universe, insidiously influences our attitude toward life. We may feel that time is running out and we must hurry to get it all done, crowd it all in, even to the point of claustrophobia in time, a feeling of oppression at the shortness of time. This sense of urgency speeds body processes—heart rate, breathing, production of certain hormones, rise in blood pressure—and can result in what Dr. Larry Dossey calls "hurry sickness" —heart disease, high blood pressure and stroke, or depression of the immune system which leads to infection, even cancer. There is no doubt that time-related anxiety can kill.[6]

According to linguist Benjamin Whorf, the Hopi Indians have quite a different view of time, one which is more in harmony with the timeless character of Duration. They have no noun for *time* and no concept of anything flowing forward or divided into segments. According to Whorf, instead, there is a general concept of change, of things enduring, of one event following another, of growing later, a concept much like that of Henri Bergson who conceived time as an unsegmented flux: " . . . true time, non-chronological time, consists of an ever-moving, eternally flowing present which contains its own past."[7] In this view time is a continuum in which lines of demarcation between past, present, and future are dissolved. Whether tied to linguistic concepts or not, a sense of flow allows us to transcend the pressures of time units and enter a stream of time in which our life can move harmoniously. It reflects the wholeness of Duration.

The Mind's Time

H.P.B., along with many philosophers, saw that time as succession of events, as sequence, is at least as much a property of our minds as it is a part of reality. We perceive serially and classify into past, present, future, while events simply "are." Time is a generalization, a concept which we abstract from concrete experience. We then give to it a life of its own, a reality on its own account, as though it had an existence apart from our experience of events. In contrast with the notion that time flows past us, who remain stationary, "left behind" by the succession of events, H.P.B. says that " 'time' is only an illusion produced by the successive states of our consciousness as *we* pass through Eternal Duration [emphasis added]."[8] Our strong tendency to order things in sequence works on our perceptions of the world, and our sense of linear time cuts up nature's unbroken panorama of intermingling changes, which is perceived more truly by the Hopi.

When we dream or fantasize or are lost in thought, time can be stretched out or telescoped, so that minutes or seconds may seem like hours or hours pass in a flash. The sense of time passing quickly or slowly can result from such physical factors as body temperature, temperature of the air, coffee, tea, alcohol, as well as from psychological factors like boredom or interest. How often we feel the work week drag by while the weekend flies! The "ordered and military progression of measured time" is very different from the "unlimited time of the mind," to use Bergson's phrases. To some people time habitually seems to flow more slowly than to others, and everyday each of us fluctuates in our perception of time's rate of flow. There are moments when time is like a stream rushing down the mountain, and then again it is like a lazy river that meanders through the plain. Neither rate is "right"; time has no absolute speed. But too much of the "rushing" can be harmful, and the slower pace can be healing.

Children are at home in nonlinear time; in play they seem to abolish measured time. Through biofeedback, meditation, creative play, and related techniques, we too can alter our sense of time and slow it down, and it has been found that biological processes are then also slowed in a healthful way.

"Hurry sickness" can be reversed by expanding our perception of time from a chronic, hectic view of an inexorable flow to a stretched-out time sense. This can be done through "time therapies" as Dr. Dossey calls them, such as visualization and imagery, biofeedback, hypnosis, and meditation. In such experiences past, present, future merge into a freedom from time's pressures, and for the moment the self-imposed domination of time over our lives is broken. These practices also tend to change our linear concept of time as relentlessly moving forward. We can learn to break the grip of linear time and experience an "eternally flowing present," perhaps sensing something of the timelessness of Duration.

When no longer dominated by clock time, by linear time, we live more in harmony with time in its cyclic guise. With people who live close to nature, the cycles of nature—the seasons, day and night, phases of the moon, spring floods—and the cycles within us—waking-sleeping, breathing, menstruation—play an important part in life. Time sense for such people is fashioned by recurrent events, their lives regulated by natural rhythms such as planting, harvesting, and milking, rather than by clocks and artificial segmentation of time. To them time appears as a never-ending dynamic process which continually returns upon itself, a spiral rather than a river. The natural rhythm of living in cyclic time is in keeping with the principle of cycles, vast and small, that theosophy and Eastern philosophy see as circling through all of manifested reality. To live in harmony with cycles is to be in harmony with the nature of the universe.

Relativity

It is not only our perception of time that varies; time itself is inconstant. Einstein's Theory of Relativity shows that time is not absolute; it speeds up and slows down. Massive bodies are known to warp space and bend light and also to slow down time. The enormous gravitational pull associated with black holes causes time to move slower and slower until time stops altogether at the surface of the "hole."

The effect of gravity can be calculated on earth by atomic clocks which measure accurately to one second in a million years. It has been found that these clocks run a bit faster high on a building than at sea level where the pull of gravity is greater. Motion also affects time: at high speeds, time slows down. Einstein pointed this out in his famous "thought" experiment in which a brother speeding around the universe in a spaceship aged far less than his twin at home on Earth. This is borne out by the fact that subatomic particles moving near the speed of light live longer than their slower counterparts. These changes in time's rate are not just psychological, nor does anything change in the clockworks. Time is actually relative to motion and to space warps.

Time also depends on the velocity and position of the observer or reference body. The relativity of time is well established in high-energy physics. As particles moving near the speed of light interact, an event may appear to occur earlier from a frame of reference nearby, later from a more distant one. The sequence of events will vary depending on the length of time it takes the light from the event to reach the observer or reference point. The concept of time speeding up and slowing is thought-provoking. It confirms our subjective experience that time does not flow at a rigid, determined rate but is variable, depending on circumstances.

Boundless Duration

Relativity theory came after H.P.B.'s time. Expounding esoteric philosophy, she viewed time as multidimensional, with many aspects depending on our level of observation. Our ideas about time, derived from our sensations, are "inextricably bound up with the relativity of human knowledge,"[9] and such ideas will vanish when we evolve to the point of seeing beyond phenomenal existence.

The boundless Duration or timelessness beyond relativity is "unconditionally eternal and universal Time," the noumenon of time, unconditioned by the phenomena which appear and disappear periodically.[10] Duration is "endless, and hence immovable . . . without beginning, without end, beyond divided Time and beyond Space."[11] It is that aspect of Reality which produces time as "the moving image of Eternity," as Plato said. The cycles of manifestation occur within this infinite Duration as the Timeless brings forth time. Thus, as with space and motion, our familiar world of divided time, of time with parts, is generated from this undivided, formless realm.

Duration embraces everything all-at-once, while experienced time must arbitrarily conform to our one-thing-at-a-time sequential view. It is hard to imagine all of reality present simultaneously in Duration, because our minds are part of the process of time. Timelessness escapes us. H.P.B. gives analogies to aid our understanding. Explaining the eternal aspect of the world, she says: "The real person or thing does not consist solely of what is seen at any particular moment, but is composed of the sum of all its various and changing conditions from its appearance in material form to its disappearance from the earth."[12] She compares these "sum-totals" to a bar of metal dropped into the sea. The present moment of a person or thing is represented by the cross section of the bar at the place where ocean and air meet. No one would say that the bar came into existence as it left the air or ceased to exist as it enters the water. So we drop out of the future into the past, momentarily presenting a cross section of ourselves in the present.

Modern physicists recognize this principle when they represent particles by world-lines, diagrams of movement through space-time. Such a line shows the direction and speed of particles and gives a more meaningful picture than would a single point, indicating but a fleeting moment in the path of the particle.

Expanding on this concept to include the world, mathematician Hermann Weyl states that "a section of [the] world comes to life as a fleeting image in space which continually changes in time."[13] David Bohm, speaking from the perspective of the holographic model, says that the whole of time may be enfolded in any given period of time. Physicist Henry Margenau views a realm where everything that we experience sequentially exists all at once in a timeless essence or universal consciousness:

> I believe that in a universal sense which is above time all events are present and real *now* . . . . We move through the all, seeing it through a slit-like window which moves along the axis of time. Perhaps the mystic has no window and is exposed indiscriminately to the universal record of the all or, to use Whitehead's phrase, to the treasure house of God's universal memory.[14]

These concepts, extrapolated from mathematics and theoretical physics, echo the timeless essence that H.P.B. called Duration. In this realm past, present, future always are; they "enter into the stream of time from an eternal world outside," as Bertrand Russell described it.[15] Natural events exist concurrently in this "world outside," but we encounter them through our time-bound minds in an ordered series of space-time slices. We cannot see the whole but only different parts one after another. I. K. Taimni, who wrote on theosophical metaphysics, perceives that "it is this seeing of different parts of a whole in succession which produces the sense of time."[16] We might think of linear time as a way our finite minds break up the wholeness of Duration into segments which we can get hold of and manage.

The vision of past, present, future as always existing might suggest determinism, like a movie reel which unrolls frame by frame in time but with the events rigidly foreordained. But this is not the implication intended. According to esoteric philosophy, existence remains fluid and dynamic, not set and predetermined. Another analogy might be a symphony, which exists complete in a timeless state. Mozart reported that his mind could seize a newly-conceived composition "at a glance"—not its various parts in succession, but all at once in its entirety. We re-enact music sequentially, a movement at a time, bar by bar, note by note. But each performance is unique. Conductors impose their individual interpretations. The tempo varies. The unforeseen happens: an orchestra member becomes ill and must be replaced at the last minute; a flute solo soars beyond any previous rendition; a drum loses the beat. There is no rigidly predetermined pattern of events in the performance, yet the symphony itself remains whole in its essential nature. Perhaps in a somewhat similar way, existence is enfolded in Duration all at once and unfolds sequentially in time, allowing the outcome some play, some freedom. It may be something like an archetype, a nonmaterial pattern or matrix which, though itself unchanging, can generate various forms, each unique but all reflecting the archetypal structure (chapter 11).

Transcending Time

We sometimes glimpse this timeless realm where past, present, and future blur into a unity, where the future "which, though it has not come into existence, still is."[17] The amazing accuracy sometimes found in prognostication, in precognition of future events, or in the occasional truly authenticated cases of past-life memory point to a world beyond our present time frame. The mystery of synchronicity, as Jung called it, the simultaneous occurrence of meaningfully related events, also jars us to consider a wider view of time and causality. Two disconnected events, one inner and one outer, converge at a meaningful moment to give us insight and growth. Why should we accidentally meet an old friend who has been through the problems we face now, or happen across a book that holds the clue to the question we have been mulling over? These experiences make us feel that we do not live in a cold, mechanical universe but that our lives have meaning. As Jungian psychologist Jean Shomoda Bolen says:

> If we personally realize that synchronicity is at work in our lives, we feel connected rather than isolated and estranged from others; we feel ourselves part of a divine, dynamic, interrelated universe.[18]

Synchronicity is another way in which the timeless whole intrudes itself into the sequence of events we experience. For, as orientalist Ananda Coomeraswamy so aptly put it, the time we know, the finite, "is not the opposite of the infinite, but only, so to speak, an excerpt from it."[19]

A universal characteristic of mystical experience is the transcendence of time, the feeling of liberation from temporality. In moments of mystic oneness, a person is lost in timeless depths which seem unbounded, which stand still. For such a person, this infinity of time exists in the immediate present, in an eternal now, not in a linear, sequential time that will run out, but in a "trysting place of mortal and immortal, time and eternity," as the poet Yeats describes it. In this experience of Duration, now and a thousand years from now are essentially the same; they are somehow both here and now in "the simultaneity of Eternity . . . in which no event has a 'when,' [but] is 'always' and 'now'."[20] The whole is in each moment as though the line of extended time collapsed into a single point which enfolds every segment of the line. In such a moment "the Past and the Future, Space and Time, disappear and become . . . the Present," as H.P.B. says.[21]

Mystics report that in communion with the Reality outside time, they feel enveloped by stillness. Time ceases to flow and move and they feel suspended in an eternal and unchanging universe of timelessness, absorbed in the immutable nature of the Transcendent Source. Though we can never grasp or understand this state with our sequential minds, there is in us at the heart of our being that which is beyond time. We have the ability to realize a timeless state, for we ourselves are essentially timeless. We issue forth from Duration and unfold our world-lines in time and space. Yet at the core we are never apart from the "still point of the turning world," as T. S. Eliot describes it. Even as we live out our days and go through the succession of events that make up our lives, "we are never in time at all, since even now we are in Eternity."[22] Through cultivating quiet, through meditation, we can come to realize our true, timeless nature and learn to reconcile it with the world of time rushing within us. As we quiet time's flow, we glimpse our roots in the timeless One.

The Unity of Motion, Space, and Time

There are moments when motion, time, and space no longer seem separate and distinct and their unity becomes apparent. In the space shuttle, seconds can mean moving over several countries; measured moments show dramatically as motion through space. Or when we look up at the sky on a clear, moonless night, we know that the light from the stars we see has traveled hundreds of thousands of light years from sources which may no longer even exist. Yet in a moment we can register the result of light moving through unimaginable distance and time. Time, space, and motion seem not just interrelated but rather different ways of looking at the same events.

Einstein showed the union of time and space in a four-dimensional continuum. The world-line of particles illustrates this; their position in space is dependent on time and vice versa. Time and space are inextricably interwoven and interdependent; only a union of the two can have independent reality. This union can be known directly in meditation. The Zen teacher Suzuki said, "As a fact of pure experience, there is no space without time, no time without space; they are interpenetrating."[23] Lama Govinda, a Tibetan Buddhist scholar, speaks of experiencing in meditation "a living continuum in which time and space are integrated."[24]

Motion, too, is an intrinsic part of this space-time unit. Time can have no meaning without something going on, without motion. The world in an unmoving state would be like the world of Sleeping Beauty in which the people froze and time stood still. Aristotle saw that time is a property of motion. To the physicist, time and space are coordinates of an event, of some form of movement. We have seen that time depends on the rate of motion. Near the speed of light, time slows down, and it speeds up for slower rates of motion. Time is the product of motion in space.

H.P.B., relating motion on the material plane to its noumenal aspect, the Great Breath, indicates this as the root of time. She speaks of the Great Breath as Absolute Existence.

Thus motion is involved with boundless time, which with infinite Space, she says, is the source of all existence. "Space and time [are] simply the forms of THAT which is the Absolute All."[25] The rich variety in the world around us is spun out from the three intertwined strands of motion, space, and time. Everything that is depends on these three.

These are not abstract metaphysical principles divorced from our practical reality. They pervade our familiar world at every point. They operate constantly in our bodies and are the backdrop of all our mental processes. And within us, as within the universe, there are timeless, spaceless depths of stillness, for "at the very heart of our being is That which is beyond all space and time, That which was, is and forever will be."[26]

II

The One Unfolding

8

The Two in One

Spirit (or consciousness) and Matter are . . . to be
regarded not as independent realities, but as the two
facets or aspects of the Absolute . . . which constitute the basis of conditioned Being, whether subjective or objective.

The Secret Doctrine

We live in a world of contrasts—light and shadow,
mountain and valley, elation and dejection, growth
and decay. The rich variety in nature and in our own inner
life results from distinctions and oppositions. Without these
life would be homogeneous, uninteresting, lacking color and
contrast, a flat experience without either joy or sorrow.

Although everything that exists is an expression of a fundamental oneness, this does not imply that all things are equal
and alike. Continuous and undifferentiated in itself, the One
nevertheless contains the possibility of all differences and opposites, an infinitude of relationships. Here at the level of
manifestation, unity expresses itself as dynamic balance, an
ever-shifting interaction between unequal parts that yet main-
tains harmony and wholeness within the process of change
and growth. Everywhere there is unity in multiplicity. Our
bodies are an example of the interplay of a variety of
specialized organ systems and processes working together as a
whole. The larger world, too, is a single living system. As

Fritjof Capra says: "The cosmos is seen as one reality, forever in motion, alive, organic, spiritual and material at the same time."[1]

Polarity Within and Without

This dynamic balance rests on the principle of polarity, a fundamental characteristic of the One which pervades all that is. The world around us is full of opposites: day and night, male and female, life and death, love and hate, inbreathing and outbreathing—the list could go on indefinitely. Polarity also pervades our perception of the world and our thinking. We view the world in terms of contrasts. Polarity is an ever-present aspect of our experience.

However, we do not often realize that we ourselves, in our perceptions, are shot through with duality. Every time we are aware of an object outside us or a thought within, we experience the basic polarity of existence. Subtly, without our realizing what is happening, the notion of the self, our consciousness, is set apart from the object or thought of which we are aware. This split between our consciousness and its contents, subject and object, pervades all our experience and at a deep level colors our most basic concept of what we are.

H.P.B. assigns all degrees and forms of consciousness to spirit: "To Spirit is referable any manifestation of consciousness." Thus *spirit and matter, consciousness and matter, subject and object* are all synonymous expressions. Spirit is not assigned a greater value than matter, its opposite. According to all schools of esoteric philosophy, they are equal, and both are basic, having their roots in the very nature of the Transcendental Source. As H.P.B. says: " . . . the opposite poles of Subject and Object, Spirit and Matter, are both aspects of the One Unity in which they are synthesized . . . ."[2] Both poles are essential for manifestation; neither could exist without the other.

The Continuum of Consciousness

Consciousness as one of the ever-present poles stems from the One Reality, which itself can be thought of as a continuum of Consciousness. In this primal, pure guise, Consciousness is unbounded, homogeneous, infinite, like Space, which is referred to in *The Secret Doctrine* as "the eternal, ever-present, Cause of all."[3] The infinity of Space can be equated with the infinity of Consciousness. Thus Consciousness in the broadest sense, as a continuum, is the One which stands behind the polar opposites of spirit (or consciousness in a narrower sense) and matter; the unbounded Continuum of Consciousness is the noumenon of the consciousness we ordinarily experience. The One Reality, the Absolute "is the *field* of Absolute Consciousness, i.e., that Essence which is out of all relation to conditioned existence, and of which conscious existence is a conditioned *symbol.*"[4]

Though the Transcendent One is homogeneous and undivided, the inscrutable Source of all, nevertheless it is not without features. H.P.B. shows us glimpses of these. She equates this nonmaterial Reality with Universal Space, which generates space; with the Great Breath, which gives rise to motion; with Duration, the father of time. Here we see another of the potentials of the One—Consciousness, which emanates both spirit and matter, our ordinary consciousness of objects as well as the objects themselves. Consciousness as the One is consciousness without an object, not consciousness *of* anything as there is no object at that level, pure, unimpeded Consciousness itself, in which yet lies the possibility of separation, of objectification. Consciousness as this undivided One is the Source of our consciousness of things, of objects, which produces our sense of multiplicity. As our minds cut up Space into small areas and Duration into measured time, so the unbroken continuum of Consciousness becomes entrapped in our nervous systems and breaks into a sense of "my consciousness" and "your consciousness."

The Poles as Interdependent

In the manifested world the two poles of consciousness and matter are inextricably intertwined at every point. Spirit or consciousness in the ordinary sense cannot exist without being grounded in some degree of materiality, and according to the esoteric teaching all matter has some degree of consciousness.

> There can be no manifestation of Consciousness, semiconsciousness, or even "unconscious purposiveness," except through the vehicle of matter . . . Both these aspects of the Absolute . . . are mutually interdependent.[5]

H.P.B. symbolizes the relation between the two poles of existence in sexual terms. Referring to the One in itself, she says, "Space [or Consciousness] is called the Mother before its cosmic activity, and Father-Mother at the first stage of reawakening."[6] She speaks of the Father as the root of consciousness and the Mother as the receptacle or matrix, the root of the material side of the world. And again she depicts the Mother (*Mulaprakriti* in Sanskrit) as a sort of veil thrown over the absolute Reality.

The Secret Doctrine explains that when the two aspects of this primal duality polarize or pull apart, so to speak, the tension between them sets up a field which gives rise to the universe, to all manifestation. The real power behind creation is a rhythmic alternation of stress or tension between the poles, a pulsating relationship between spirit and matter. This concept is poetically expressed in the Stanzas of Dzyan, on which *The Secret Doctrine* is based:

> Father-Mother spin a web whose upper end is fastened to
> Spirit—the light of the one darkness — and the lower one
> to its shadowy end, matter; and this web is the universe
> spun out of the two substances made in one.[7]

The mystery of how the tension between the two poles gives rise to the manifold world with its endless variety is a fruitful subject for contemplation. An ordinary magnet gives us hints about the dynamics of this fundamental polarity. The strong attractions and repulsions of the field surrounding a magnet govern the behavior of iron particles sprinkled in the field, and they take on pattern and organization. Perhaps similarly, the universe latent in the One takes shape through the dynamic interplay of the two poles of spirit and matter.

Subject-Object

We have seen that these poles exist in us, intermingled at the base of our being. H.P.B. explains that our consciousness comes from spirit (the Father) and is encased in several vehicles of varying density which comes from Cosmic Substance (the Mother) (chapter 17). Any thought, feeling, sensation we may experience results from a blend of the two poles of consciousness and matter, subject and object. We, as the conscious experiencer, feel separate from the object that we experience. We identify with an inner self, an innermost consciousness, which separates itself from external objects and even from our own thoughts and feelings. Yet the two poles of subject and object in us are mutually interdependent; neither could exist without the other, as the positive pole of a magnet could not exist without the negative. Both poles pervade our every experience.

We can sense the perpetual interplay between the poles in ourselves. Every time we move a muscle, our consciousness intervenes in the world of matter. The interaction of consciousness and matter underlies all our sensory experience—vision, hearing, tactile sense, etc. Impressions impinging on our sense organs set off electrical and chemical impulses which travel along nerves to the brain. Perhaps the greatest mystery of all to psychologists is the way these impulses become translated into conscious experience, so that we consciously see, hear, or feel the outer stimulus. Yet this interaction of consciousness and matter goes on within us constantly. Medical science is becoming increasingly aware of the effect of consciousness on the body and on health. High blood pressure, ulcers, epilepsy, migraine, and cancer are only a few of the illnesses that can respond to "consciousness therapies" such as biofeedback, visualization, and meditation, in which changes in consciousness affect the disease process.[8]

Consciousness in Matter

The blending of the poles is found throughout nature. According to *The Secret Doctrine*, everything is a combination of spirit or consciousness and matter. Even so-called inert matter has a degree of consciousness or responsiveness.

> Everything in the Universe, through all its kingdoms, is conscious: i.e., endowed with a consciousness of its own kind and on its own plane of perception. We men must remember that, simply because *we* do not perceive any signs which we can recognize—of consciousness—say, in stones, we have no right to say that *no consciousness exists there.* There is no such thing as either "dead" or "blind" matter, as there is no "blind" or "unconscious" Law.[9]

The idea of life or consciousness in all matter is gaining credence with some scientists. Teilhard de Chardin wrote of the "within of things," the inner, conscious side of everything, animate or inanimate. He held that because consciousness exists at all, it must exist everywhere, even in minerals, in some rudimentary form, and that consciousness is enriched and enhanced through evolution. Another modern view in harmony with theosophy rests on the presence of consciousness throughout the world of life. Intelligence exists without a brain in primitive forms of life, even in one-celled organisms. There is no point in the development of an embryo where mind comes into being. There is no organ or local site in organisms which is necessary for consciousness to emerge. Life sprang from the intricate combination of molecules. To some scientists this implies that consciousness must be implicit in matter itself, that all matter holds the possibility of life or consciousness or mind. According to biologist Erich Jantsch, "If consciousness is defined as the degree of autonomy a system gains in the dynamic relations with its environment, even the simplest . . . systems such as chemical . . . structures have a primitive form of consciousness."[10] The late eminent psychologist Gardner Murphy felt that this does not disparage humanity, in whom consciousness has flowered, but rather "glorifies the primal ooze."

Thus some degree of responsiveness exists in every form. H.P.B. tells us that "Nature, taken in its abstract sense, *cannot* be 'unconscious,' as it is the emanation from, and thus an aspect . . . of, the Absolute consciousness."[11] People who work with crystals in healing become aware of a kind of living quality in them which differs with different minerals. Responsiveness in plants is shown in their tropisms, as their shoots reach for the sun and their roots sink into the soil. Some studies have shown that they also respond to music and to human emotions. Consciousness and responsiveness are self-evident in animals and humans. The potentiality of consciousness is released in a myriad of forms. Sometimes matter predominates as in minerals; sometimes consciousness is most prominent, as in humans. Every form is a blend of the two poles which permeate all nature and which are an essential part of all that exists. "The Manifested Universe . . . is pervaded by duality, which is, as it were, the very essence of its EX-istence . . ."[12]

Reflected Polarities

We have seen how fundamental principles of esoteric philosophy are reflected everywhere in nature. Unity and wholeness, motion, space and time appear over and over in the world, manifestations of the eternal noumenal principles. We are tempted to assume that the many polarities in ourselves and in the physical world must somehow reflect the basic polarity between spirit or consciousness and matter. Subject-object, or consciousness-matter, would seem to be the prototype of the countless dualisms we see throughout nature, the fundamental poles, with all other opposites in the world but shadows of this basic split. However, H.P.B. has little to say in this regard. Whereas in writing about motion and the Great Breath, she relates it to movements in the manifested world, in explaining the poles she hardly refers to the principle of polarity in its many guises all around us. She does occasionally mention the attraction of opposites—as in static electricity, in gravity, in the attraction between the sexes—as a kind of physical polarity and includes repulsion between similar polarities.

It would seem that all the strong, active, masculine polarities in the world reflect the potential of spirit, while the receptive, passive, feminine ones reflect the qualities of matter. The fact that H.P.B. chose Father and Mother to sym-

bolize consciousness and matter shows the affinity of the
sexual principle with the ultimate polarity.

Positive and negative, male and female, active and passive
poles are deep-rooted in the nature of reality and are essential
to manifestation. Positive and negative charges at the subatomic level of matter undergird the entire physical world.
The innumerable substances and varieties of materials rest on
valence, on the electrons and protons within atoms and their
interactions in molecules. Modern physicists believe so
strongly in polarity that they even posit antimatter; for every
particle there is an antiparticle of equal and opposite charge.

Prem and Ashish carry the concept of attraction and repulsion farther, indicating that the striving of subject toward object, the mutual attraction between the poles of consciousness
and matter, is characteristic of desire, which is tied to its opposite, repulsion. A little introspection will reveal the power
of these two forces of attraction and repulsion in us. Our likes
and dislikes, attractions and aversions—based on another
pair of opposites, pleasure and pain—generate more of our
actions than we might suppose. Polarity is a powerful force in
our lives and in all living creatures.

It is obvious that the polarity of the sexes is essential in the
world of living things and our human world. In addition to
ensuring the continuance of our species, it lends drama and
variety to our experience. Male-female relations are by far the
most popular subject for art and literature, movies and television, and romantic thoughts dominate a great many people.

As spirit and matter always occur together and are never
found apart from one another, so both male and female
polarities exist within each of us. We all experience tender-
ness, softness, yielding, as well as decisiveness, aggressive-
ness, strength. The feminine in us is often equated with intuition, while the orderly, rational mind is thought of as
masculine. These poles correspond in general to the functions
of the right and left hemispheres of the brain. The
psychologist Abraham Maslow has pointed out that truly
mature people incorporate opposite poles in their natures.
Self-actualizers, as he called them, can accept help and com-

fort from others as well as give it, are sometimes strong and at other times yielding. They are well-rounded and complete.

Alternating poles, opposites, and contrasts are prominent within our natures. Our moods constantly swing between depression and elation, love and hate or resentment, hunger and satiation, anxiety and confidence, energy and fatigue. It is natural for each pole to be replaced by its opposite. The many polarities in us, such as conscious-unconscious, mental-emotional, persona-shadow, are necessary for our wholeness. For complete expression of what we are, we should not try to eliminate any one pole and perfect the other. That would be like "following and honoring Heaven with no account of Earth," as Chuang Tzu put it. Rather we should admit both poles and strike a dynamic balance between them. Eliminating one, or trying to, only truncates our being.

Opposites Intertwined

As with spirit and matter, the myriad poles in the world are not separate from one another but express two aspects of a surrounding whole. They show relative contrasts within an all-embracing unity, the extremes of a continuum. Figure-ground, up-down, hot-cold, back-front—in innumerable pairs each pole depends on the other for its existence; they have meaning only in relation to one another. Alan Watts perceived this unity in opposites:

> To say opposites are polar—is to say that they are related and joined—that they are terms, ends, extremities of a single whole. Polar opposites are inseparable opposites . . . [13]

In addition, many opposites turn into one another in endless succession. H.P.B. stressed the importance of such cycles (chapter 12). Prem and Ashish perceive the Great Breath as the driving power behind cycles, a constant pulsation which results in a rhythmic alternation of tension between the poles. Because of this pulse, "nothing is ever in a static state of rest, but is forever changing and 'passing into its opposite.' "[14] We see this when day becomes night as the earth turns on its axis, so that night and day are but phases of a single process. Summer-winter, ebb-flow, sleeping-waking, inbreathing-out-breathing are other examples. Even life and death, in the theosophical and Eastern view, are poles of a continuous process. According to Alan Watts, "Life and death are not so much alternatives as alternations, poles of a single process, which may be called life-and-death."[15]

The ancient Taoist doctrine of Yin and Yang portrays op-posites as intertwined, with each pole containing the seed of the other, as shown in the familiar Yin-Yang symbol. The Yang aspect symbolizes that which is light, strong, male,

forceful, active, heavenly, while Yin is dark, yielding, female, passive, earthly. In life situations these are seen as alternating with one another in continuous rhythm, becoming one another, as do night and day. Their dynamic balance is beautifully portrayed in *T'ai Chi,* the Chinese exercise-dance, in which each forceful, strong motion gives way to one which is soft and yielding, only to be replaced again by strength.

Mental Dualities

The separation between poles does not exist in nature but results from the tendency of our minds, particularly the Western mind, to separate things and place them in airtight compartments, giving them labels which further solidify the distinctions. Our two-term logic demands that something is this *or* that, one or the other, whereas the Eastern view tends to encompass both. We usually make sharp, clear-cut categories and then assume that nature matches our concepts. Many opposites are only relative, as a stick may appear short in comparison to a longer one, or long compared to a short one. Our minds dichotomize and set up dualities through which we then view the unbroken wholeness of nature. Many opposites are only abstract concepts belonging to the world of thought.

The great Danish physicist Niels Bohr acknowledged the Taoist concept of Yin and Yang and saw the harmony between Eastern wisdom and modern Western science. He introduced the concept of complementarity to unify opposites and accommodate the many disparities in physics. Einstein showed the unity of two seemingly disparate things—matter and energy—in his formula $E = Mc^2$. Electrons, which appear as both particles and waves, can also be considered to be both, in some as yet incomprehensible way. To the nuclear physicist matter seems both destructible and indestructible, continuous and discontinuous, and manifests itself in many ways that seem to be mutually exclusive. Bohr felt that the framework of distinct and separate opposites is too narrow to accommodate nature, that the incompatibilities are the product of our minds and observations rather than inherent in nature. For him waves and particles are complementary aspects of the same reality, each a limited and partial view and both needed to give a complete picture. Thus he perceived the theosophical principle that poles inhere together in a larger whole.

Physicists have rediscovered another insight of esoteric philosophy—that subject and object cannot be divorced from one another. We in the West have dichotomized the two, especially ever since the 17th century when the philosopher Descartes insisted that the material world is objective and forever split off from human consciousness. In the process of trying to know reality as an object, we have thought of ourselves, the subject, as fundamentally separate and distinct

from all else. In recent decades physicists happened on an insight that shows this split between subject and object to be
mistaken. In quantum physics they found that the scientists
who measure can never completely separate themselves from
what is being measured.[16] For example, the tools used for
measuring electrons are photons, very small subatomic particles. But photons cause electrons to change position ever so
slightly. Thus the observer, in his subjective concepts and instruments, interacts with the observed. Many feel that quantum physics is not a special case, that the whole process of
trying to posit reality as entirely objective and external is
futile, that the mind and consciousness always intervene.
Physicist John Wheeler speaks of a "participatory universe" in
which human consciousness necessarily interacts, even when
trying only to observe. Ken Wilber perceives the unity of the
subject with its object: "Just as front and back are simply two
ways of viewing one body, so subject and object, psyche and
soma, energy and matter are but two ways of approaching
one reality."[17] As *The Secret Doctrine* holds, consciousness
and matter are forever intertwined in a larger whole.

Rising Above the Opposites

However, in spite of this perspective in esoteric philosophy
and in physics, we have a deep unconscious habit of separating ourselves as subject from all else as object. This results
in our seeing ourselves as separated, isolated islands of awareness. There is another way of looking at ourselves and the
world, a mode of knowing that does not separate the knower
from the known, the subject from the object. Sages East and
West have reached a perspective from which they see clearly
that all polar opposites are relative. The aim of Eastern traditions is to realize the unity of opposites, to "be in truth eternal, beyond earthly opposites," as the *Bhagavad Gita* says.
This realization is achieved by subduing intellectual distinctions and emotional polarities so that the unity of opposites
becomes a vivid experience.

There are any number of methods of meditation and techniques for heightening awareness which can help us rise

above the opposites. They all involve quieting the divisive, polarizing mind and reaching our innermost consciousness, which underlies all modes of thinking and feeling. What would it be like if the body could be completely quiet with no sensory input, not the slightest sight or sound or sense of touch or pressure or heat or cold? Also the emotions would subside and leave not a trace of excitement, affection, anger, or anxiety. The mind, too, would stop its flow and all thoughts would die out. What would be left? We would come close to experiencing consciousness without an object, without any content, bare awareness. Though in our human condition it is impossible to experience consciousness completely apart from our vehicles, physical or superphysical, we would sense something of the boundless continuum of pure Consciousness. We would see, with Carlo Suares, that in consciousness "there are no insular compartments, no partitions or dividing walls."

Such an act of letting go of everything familiar, of all that we have thought ourselves to be, of every support that gives us a sense of security, is called *the leap* in mystical literature. At first it can be terrifying, as one's whole self seems to be obliterated into nothingness. However, those who have penetrated this state and have come to be at home in it report that it does not annihilate their being but rather revolutionizes their understanding of what they are. Even after sinking back into an ordinary state, they can no longer completely identify with their old concept of self. They know that the split between subject and object, knower and known, is illusory. The self and the world are no longer seen as separate but rather united in a field of undivided Consciousness, that unity from which both subject and object arise. To think of "my consciousness" becomes absurd, as there is only Consciousness, an unbounded continuum that cannot be divided, "a singular of which the plural is unknown," as physicist Erwin Schroedinger has described it. By loosening the bonds of ordinary consciousness, we get intimations of the field of Consciousness, the one ground that links all polarities, that "nameless nothingness" of which the mystic Eckhart spoke. And yet the nothingness is not a blank vacuum but pure joy, not based on any outer circumstance, but simply boundless joy that wells up from deep within and spills over in ever-widening circles, spreading out in Space.

The Ultimate Polarity

This experience of pure consciousness without an object places one beyond subject and object and beyond all the world's polarities. Yet, paradoxically, another polarity becomes apparent at this level. The *Upanishads* say that the pure consciousness (*Atman* in Sanskrit) is "smaller than the small," yet "greater than the great." This enigma rests on the ability of the One to be a continuous, unbroken whole and at the same time to be many individuals. *The Secret Doctrine* uses the analogy of numberless sparks in one flame to represent this enigma. A point in the center of a circle is also suggestive. While the Transcendent Source encompasses boundless Space, it is also focused in innumerable points which are the core consciousness of individuals.

Experience in meditation confirms the esoteric teaching of the individual as contiguous with the whole. In moments of deep inwardness, many meditators report an expansion and widening of consciousness that coincides with a centering, as though one's consciousness were implanted in a point deep inside and yet somehow spread out to encompass all. We are simultaneously smaller than the small and greater than the great. We might get some faint insight into this mystery by contemplating a dandelion gone to seed. The wholeness of its fragile globe radiates from a central core; the all-encompassing sphere and the deep center are part of one whole. This image might capture some aspects of a state of pure consciousness, and suggest how the all-pervasive principle of polarity operates even in the highest states.

9

Rhythm and Cycles

Everything that lives seems to be expressive of a
rhythmic motion . . . . It is the visible outflow of an
invisible divine order, which embraces man and
nature alike.

Edith Schnapper, *The Inward Odyssey*

*E*very night stars circle the firmament around the earth;
with each beat the heart alternately shrinks and swells in
ceaseless rhythm; water rises in vapor, forms clouds, and falls
back to earth as rain; seeds become shoots, flowers turn to
fruit, fruit begets seeds—all these reveal the grand principle of
cyclicity. Cycles are so universal in nature that the law of
periodicity is the second of the three Fundamental Proposi-
tions in *The Secret Doctrine,* the first being the doctrine of the
Transcendent One. H.P.B. explains that the cycles we see
everywhere in nature and in ourselves are expressions of this
basic law, which she refers to as "one of the absolutely fundamental laws of the universe."

As with the other universals we have considered, the principle of cyclicity has its origin in the Transcendental Source.
The metaphysical foundation of cycles is interaction between
the poles of spirit and matter. The prototype of all lesser

cycles is the inbreathing and outbreathing of universes from the One. This doctrine holds that the present cosmos, ancient as it is, was preceded by an endless series of earlier manifestations. There are immense intervals in which the pole of consciousness or spirit predominates and all is quiescent in a silent, indrawn state of potentiality called *pralaya*. Then, as emanation of the universe-to-be begins, the pole of matter is activated in a phase called *manvantara*. As manifestation proceeds, the material side becomes more and more predominant until the apex of materiality is reached. Then the pole of consciousness or spirit again slowly takes the ascendency, as all moves toward another pralaya. As one pole waxes, the other wanes (chapter 12). Thus, periods of cosmic activity are followed by dark periods of non-being in which life dies down to the basic heartbeat of a resting state. *The Secret Doctrine* refers to this cosmic cycle as the Great Breath, which proceeds from "the One Life which itself is eternal . . . without beginning or end, yet periodical in its regular manifestations."[1]

We might imagine how the poles pulling apart, so to speak, activate the initial rhythm in the world being formed. A field analogous to the field around a magnet springs into being between the two poles. Tension results, setting up a dynamism that disrupts the static state. The forces of attraction and repulsion cause an alternating pulse between the poles.

This metaphysical principle might be illustrated by a simple generator in which electricity is produced by magnetism. As a coil of wire revolves between the two poles of a magnet, it cuts across the lines of magnetic force in the field, causing an electric current to flow through the wire. The current flows first in one direction as it approaches one pole in its revolving and then reverses as it approaches the other. The resulting alternating current reflects the polarity, the attraction and repulsion, within the magnetic field. This process might reflect in some measure the way in which cycles are produced by the dynamic counterpoint between the two poles of Being. Perhaps H.P.B. meant something like this when she said "Motion . . . assumes an ever-growing tendency . . . to circular movement."[2]

This eternal rhythm of outflow and return, inwardness and outwardness, is reflected everywhere in nature. The pattern is so widespread that H.P.B held the "absolute universality of that law of periodicity" to be self-evident. Prem and Ashish stress this alternation:

> Everywhere throughout the whole realm of nature, physical or psychic, from atoms to universes . . . a period of expansion is followed by one of contraction, a period of running down by one of winding up.[3]

Ocean waves and foot steps display the cyclic principle that pervades all nature.

Rhythm, which pervades nature and is in everything we experience, is based on the principle of alternation. The inrush and outrush of air with each breath, the development from the latency of a seed to the full growth of a plant, the withdrawal of sleep and activity of waking, the upbeat and downbeat of birds' wings, all these show an active and a resting phase, a swing between two poles. Rhythm is involved in most of our activities—walking, talking, sexual activity, sports—but perhaps it is most obvious in music and dancing. These rhythmic activities are found in all cultures, with something analogous appearing even among animals. Whether the rhythm is simple, like an elementary drumbeat or the neck-dipping in courting swans, or is complex and intricate, like a symphony or an Indian raga, it all stems from the fundamental rhythmicity of alternating poles, upbeat-downbeat, strong-weak, active-resting. Simple rhythms might comprise simple cycles, or they might intermesh to create more complex cycles.

All the metaphysical principles we have considered enter into rhythm and cycles. Time is intrinsic to rhythm, as to all movement, as rhythmic processes must flow through time. Space and motion, too, are basic to cycles; we cannot imagine rhythm without something moving, something which has extension in space. Rhythm could not appear in a frozen, motionless state.

Emily Sellon, student of *The Secret Doctrine*, sums up this relationship between polarity, motion, and space-time:

> The dynamic polar relationship between (the poles) of consciousness and matter imparts to the universe its fundamental, ever-present motion, whose on-going character instills a rhythmic order or periodicity, giving birth to time. This manifests itself throughout nature as the space-time processes of birth and death, the cycles of growth and decay. This, the basic life-action of the universe, is called the Great Breath.[4]

Cycles Great and Small

All these principles—motion, time, space, polarity—are as much involved in our every heartbeat and in the life cycle of even the tiniest creature as they are in the emergence and dissolution of universes. Like the other principles discussed, cycles are so universal and omnipresent that we do not usually notice them. Yet they underlie our experience at every level of being. On the large scale in nature, cycles undergird ecosystems, as gases and minerals are exchanged through the various organisms in the system. Some cycles are very long. Civilizations come and go in a matter of hundreds or thousands of years. The precession of the equinoxes, in which the celestial background of stars and constellations turns full circle in the heavens around the earth, takes over 25,000 years. The birth and death of stars may take billions of years.

Innumerable cycles, long and short, are keyed to the "circular" movement of orbits and rotations of heavenly bodies. The seasons, resulting from the earth's orbit around the sun, have governed man's life since earliest times when the rhythm of planting and harvesting first set the pattern for annual events. Animals migrate, mate, give birth according to this yearly cycle. The hatching of a baby bird is programmed by the earth's relation to the sun 93 million miles away.

The 24-hour period of the earth's rotation on its axis is keyed to numberless circadian or daily rhythms in living things. Waking and sleeping are the most obvious. In addition, the body goes through any number of daily cycles such as the rise and fall of hormone production, changes in the rate of breathing, heart rate, rhythms of brain waves, peaks and valleys of body heat. There are also many smaller rhythms within us, such as the 90-minute cycle in which light sleep alternates with deep, dreaming sleep. Cycles occur within each cell. Mitosis, the doubling of cells to form new cells, is cyclic, its rate depending on the function of the cell in the body. The rate of metabolism or the burning of foods in cells is also cyclic.

Harmony through Breathing

According to theosophy, these cycles within our bodies illustrate our intimate connection with the Transcendent Source, for they reflect the rhythm of the Great Breath which is at the root of all cycles. Breathing particularly exemplifies this powerful principle in nature and symbolizes universal interactions. This vital function, essential for life, dramatizes the way nature's cycles are interlocked and intermeshed at many levels. In breathing the circulatory system works in tandem with the respiratory system as the heart pumps freshly oxygenated blood from the lungs to all parts of the body. On its return trip the blood picks up carbon dioxide, a waste product, from the cells and delivers it for expulsion by the lungs. The brain and central nervous system, the body chemistry and the metabolic processes are all closely synchronized with breathing. They in turn effect processes in tissues and glands. Breathing keys into our entire bodily system, and is even involved with emotional states. In us and in all living things, life is governed by the action of cycles within cycles, which must be synchronized like clockwork for our survival.

Breathing has a central place for another reason. It is pivotal between various sets of opposites within us: conscious-unconscious, individual-environment, inside-outside, awareness-body, individual-universal. Breath does not merely swing between these opposites but rather integrates many levels.

We continually exchange with the environment through breath, as we inhale and expel gases. In the process, that which was outside is taken in, and that which is within is breathed out. According to yoga philosophy, in addition to gases we absorb a vital energy called *prana* from the atmosphere as we breathe. Theosophy recognizes prana as a universal life force flowing throughout nature, which nourishes and vivifies all living things. It is deeply involved in health. Thus breathing is a means for perpetual exchange with this vital superphysical energy.

Breathing goes on unconsciously for the most part, but we can consciously intervene in its rhythm at any time. It is crucial for us to have this ability as breath is the foundation of speech. We must modify and control our breath every time we speak or sing, laugh or sigh. Thus breath links mind, the source of speech, with body, through which it is expressed.

Also, breathing and conscious states are closely interlinked, and our breathing changes with emotional and physiological states. Breath comes faster when we exercise or are emotionally aroused. It is shallow when we are tense or anxious and deepens in sleep or states of deep calm or meditation. We can exert some control over these states by deliberately controlling our rate and manner of breathing. In many systems of meditation breathing is central. Pranayama, the practice of controlled breathing in yoga, prescribes various breathing exercises to energize the body, quiet the emotions, and reach an inner calm and steadiness in which there is a flow of universal forces. Lama Govinda points out:

> Breathing becomes a vehicle of spiritual experience, the mediator between body and mind. It is the first step toward the transformation of the body from the state of a more or less passively and unconsciously functioning physical organ into a vehicle or tool of a perfectly developed and enlightened mind.[5]

He teaches that breathing can lead to "perfect mental and physical equilibrium and its resulting inner harmony (out of which) grows that serenity and happiness which fills the whole body with a feeling of supreme bliss, like the refreshing coolness of a spring that penetrates the entire water of a mountain lake."[6]

Though breathing begins as an unconscious process, it can be consciously cultivated to lead to high states of super-conscious experience. It can be the means of conscious union with the universal, the personal self with the spiritual. Through breath, we as individuals constantly exchange with our surroundings on physical, superphysical, and spiritual levels. Through our breath we are sustained at every moment by a larger environment which supports all aspects of our life. The rhythm of our breathing is harmonious with the or-chestration of the cosmic Breath, keeping us alive at every level by a constant interchange with the whole.

Cycles Intermeshed

The harmonization of our breath with numberless cycles within us and around us can be taken as a symbol of a princi-ple that operates throughout nature. The Hermetic axiom "as above, so below" applies here. H.P.B. painted a picture of cycles within cycles that is reminiscent of the holistic view of wholes within wholes. Nature and its numberless cycles might be compared to a great symphony with each cycle having its unique place in the ongoing rhythm of the whole. From cell division to the rise and fall of civilizations, each cycle fits into the larger rhythms of the earth and the cosmos. Every individual cycle is correlated and intermeshed with the flow of a harmonious overarching pattern. H.P.B. expresses this idea:

> Cycles merging into cycles, containing and contained in an endless series. The embryo evolving in his prenatal sphere, the individual in his family, the family in the state, the state in mankind, the earth in our system, that system in its central universe, the universe in the Kosmos, the Kosmos in the One Cause—
> All are but parts of one stupendous whole,
> Whose body nature is and God the soul.[7]

According to esoteric philosophy, the pattern of cycles is not confined to the physical world but is repeated at every level of being. There are cycles at mental and spiritual levels in us and in the larger pattern of the cosmos. Individually we are subject to rhythmic mental and spiritual unfoldment and civilizations and races of men also follow this law. Mankind as a whole moves forward according to cycles. H.P.B. makes this clear when she says:

> The Cycles of Matter will be succeeded by Cycles of Spirituality and a fully developed mind . . . . Humanity is the child of cyclic Destiny, and not one of its Units can escape its unconscious mission, or get rid of the burden of its cooperative work with nature. Thus will mankind, race after race, perform its appointed cycle-pilgrimage.[8]

Progress through Cycles

Progress is possible through cycles because they are not rigid and purely repetitive. Time imparts a direction to the movement, an ongoing continuity in which the phases of cycles are stretched out sequentially. Thus, all cycles are characterized by a regular pattern of ordered progression through phases based on rhythm.

Nevertheless, cycles do not simply duplicate one another; each is unique. Though structurally they all follow a basic form of cyclic order, they respond to varying conditions within themselves and in the environment. This is obvious in examining the growth rings of a tree which are built up year by year as the tree grows. Variations in the rings reflect that year's drought or plentiful rainfall, the severity of the winter, etc. Even quick cycles such as the heartbeat can vary from moment to moment, from fast and fluttering to slow and steady. No cycle exactly repeats the preceding one. Prem and Ashish call attention to this variation when they speak of eternally recurring cycles as "vast systems of cyclic order, cycles that are regularly recurrent in general, though infinitely variable in particulars."[9]

Theosophy depicts the cycles as ascending and recurring at a higher level each time around, not an endless circle that goes nowhere, but a spiral of growth. The never-ceasing process of cycles continually returns upon itself, but not necessarily to the starting point. Dane Rudhyar, a philosopher-astrologer who has written several books on the principle of cyclicity, perceives that the spiral rather than the straight line is the symbol of progress. The backward turn of the spiral may seem to reverse the direction, but it is necessary for the upward movement. He views the spiral not as going smoothly and continuously uphill, but as the act of walking, with a series of falls and recoveries. H.P.B. refers to the ascent through upward and downward movements as "the immutable law of Nature which is Eternal Motion, cyclic and spiral—therefore progressive even in its seeming retrogression."[10] This upward spiralling of the cycles results in evolution, as we shall see in chapter 12.

Build-up and Decline

As cycles swing between their inward- and outward-turned phases, they produce a pattern of birth, rapid development, peak, decline, and death. The falling phase is as much a part of nature as the rise; both are intrinsic to the inexorable cyclic progression. Forms are built up, grow, and flourish. But even during growth, the forces of withdrawal are present, and they become dominant in the later phases. Both processes go on continually in our bodies as anabolism in our cells builds the body by changing food into living tissues, while catabolism tears tissue down into waste products. Both processes are necessary for life. The earth itself undergoes similar changes; volcanoes build up the surface while erosion wears it down. In living organisms these phases of creation and decay tend to follow each other in sequence, though with overlap. Dane Rudhyar perceives the rising and receding activity of two forces: "Life is a cyclic interplay of polar energies . . . . The waning of the energy of one pole . . . is always associated with the waxing in strength of the other pole."[11]

Each of us must experience birth, childhood, adolescence, maturity, old age, and death. The phases of our life cycles have psychological counterparts. In the earlier phases there is expansion and reaching out, both physically and psychologically. The later phases are characterized by consolidation and withdrawal. Rites of passage are held to mark crucial points between phases—birth, coming of age, marriage, death. These transitions have profound impact on all of us, and many people find them traumatic.

Civilizations, too, follow phases of growth and decay, as Toynbee and others have attempted to show. The tremendous upheavals going on in every field today are seen by some as the birth pangs of a new age. Even stars follow a pattern of youth, maturity, old age, and finally death. They evolve from an inchoate cloud of gas to a globe of fire in which internal processes produce unimaginable explosions of nuclear power. These globes flare up then stabilize as in our sun, and finally reach a point of implosion after which the star disappears. But new clouds of gas sometimes collect at the site of a long-dead star, to begin the process over again.

Thus rise and fall, creation and destruction, are natural phases of the cyclic order. We see this every year in the cycle of the seasons when winter's withdrawal of life and seeming death are followed by a burst of new life in spring. In the West we tend to value the constructive phase and fear destruction, but in the East both are seen as necessary and natural. In Hindu symbology both appear as primary gods, equal to one another—Brahma the Creator and Shiva the Destroyer. Alan Watts describes the dance in Hindu mythology in which the ten-armed Shiva, wreathed in fire, destroys the universe at the end of each cycle. But Shiva is simply the opposite face of Brahma the Creator, so that as he turns to leave with the world in ruin, the scene changes with

his turning, and all things are seen to have been remade under the cover of their destruction.[12]

Man's Cycle

According to esoteric philosophy, just as universes are outbreathed and inbreathed, we too undergo a cycle of forthgoing and return in the form of a long series of rebirths and reincarnations interspersed with periods of gestation. Our being pulses with the ongoing process of the Great Breath. H.P.B. refers to this as the "cycle of necessity . . . the obligatory pilgrimage for every soul . . . through the cycles of Incarnation in accordance with Cyclic and Karmic law."[13] In the theosophical view, death is not an end but only a necessary phase in the greater cycle of life. Death is seen as merely a quiescent interval in which the subjective pole predominates for a time between physical embodiments.

After each of these periods, the outgoing, active pole of objectivity overwhelms the subjective phase once again as the pilgrim soul embarks on a new physical adventure. Even as a tree takes on new life each spring, we undergo an endless series of new beginnings. We follow nature's spiral pattern as we continue to unfold and grow through the ups and downs of many lifetimes. We are one with that far-reaching pattern of cyclicity, which provides us with the means for never-ending growth and unfoldment. The metaphysical principles that inhere in the Transcendent One are reflected in us, as throughout the cosmos at every level.

When we become aware of the natural order of rhythmic cycles, we can translate this realization into greater acceptance and understanding of our lives. In a cycle each phase is where it should be in the whole process. The stages of life are natural and inevitable. We need not fight life's transitions, ever-increasing independence from parents, choosing a mate, the midlife crisis, old age, even death. Each phase has its proper place in the overall pattern, and each has its lessons and opportunities for new growth. We can come to relish each stage of life as Thoreau tells us to relish the seasons:

> Live in each season as it passes; breathe the air, drink the drink, taste the fruit, and resign yourself to the influences of each . . . . Be blown on by all the winds. Open all your pores and bathe in all the tides of Nature, in all her streams and oceans, at all seasons . . . grow green with spring, yellow and ripe with autumn. Drink of each season's influence as a vial, a true panacea of all remedies mixed for your special use.[14]

Yet, even as we swing with life's rhythms and learn to open ourselves to each phase, at a deeper level we are not truly within the cycles. In the midst of the whirling and changing worlds, we are ever rooted in the One, our deepest center of consciousness grounded in that unchanging, eternal background. We are the still, small point that stands behind all life's movements, the center of the wheel around which all turns but which itself is motionless. If we come to experience

this core of stillness within through meditation and centering, then even as life's circumstances rise and fall, we can remain calm and serene, balanced at the fulcrum point that remains steady as life teeters around us.

10

Divine Mind

> [The scientist's] religious feeling takes the form of a
> rapturous amazement at the harmony of natural law,
> which reveals an intelligence of such superiority that,
> compared with it, all the systematic thinking and
> acting of human beings is an utterly insignificant
> reflection.
>
> Albert Einstein

*T*hroughout history poets and philosophers have been
awed by the geometry of nature. The designs in the
curve of a seashell or spiral nebula, the pattern of petals in a
blossom, a spider's web, the fluting formed by the sea on the
sand—these all reveal geometric symmetry. Perhaps even
more remarkable is ordered sequencing through time, as in
the stages of cells dividing, with the duplication of all the intricate microscopic parts in precise sequence. The growth of
an embryo is an even more complex masterpiece of delicately
timed stages. The order which nature shows in such abundance elicited scientist-philosopher James Jeans's famous
statement: "The universe is . . . like a thought of a mathematical thinker."

The "mathematical thinker" in theosophical terms is the
Divine Mind, what H.P.B. calls "the basis of the intelligent
operations in and of Nature." It is Universal Intelligence, the
organizing, structuring principle at work behind nature, im-

posing order and purpose on the entire cosmic process. This aspect of the creative nonmaterial Reality is characterized by law and harmony and, according to *The Secret Doctrine*, "supplies the guiding intelligence in the vast scheme of Cosmic Evolution."[1] As the world of form emerges from the undifferentiated One, this divine Intelligence implants intrinsic order, proportion, harmony in nature's self-ordering systems. The forms of nature are exteriorized representations of Divine Thought, which induces direction and organization in what had been inchoate and vague precosmic matter. This principle of intelligence "enters into" and "agitates" matter, shaping it according to laws of harmony as it fashions the world. "Apart from Cosmic Ideation, Cosmic Substance would remain an empty abstraction."[2]

H.P.B. refers to Universal Mind as "the one *impersonal* Great Architect of the Universe." However, she stresses that this "architect" is not outside the Cosmos, imposing order on it; it is not a creator apart from creation like a sculptor shaping clay. Rather the Divine Mind is intrinsic in nature, an innate part of natural processes, giving coherence and intelligent inner direction to natural forms.

Theosophy, along with Plato, teaches that all beauties of the earth have their source in the Divine Mind. Einstein glimpsed this. He was in awe of the "sublimity and marvelous order" of the universe and "the marvelous structure of reality." He seems to have intuited the living quality of the Divine Mind which he called "the mysterious" when he spoke of

> a knowledge of the existence of something we cannot penetrate, of the manifestations of the profoundest reason and the most radiant beauty, which are only accessible to our reason in their most elementary forms.[3]

This exquisitely precise noumenal principle of order referred to by Einstein is also expressed in the Hermetic saying that describes the world: "Out of the Infinite Deep's universe a work of art has been conceived and brought to birth, an ensouled work of art."[4] Concrete expressions of order echo this sublime Source.

Enfolded in the One

The Divine Mind, like the other metaphysical principles, stems from the very nature of the One. All these principles—unity, time, space, motion, polarity—are enfolded in the One from the beginning, not like Chinese boxes nested in one another, but more like characteristics of the adult latent in the embryo. They inhere simultaneously in the One and become activated as the cycle of manifestation proceeds. Prem and Ashish allude to the process by which the Divine Mind is manifested: "The unmanifest principles of being separate from their state of primal fusion and give birth to the manifest glory of Universal Mind."[5]

The Universal Mind is the first *manifested* principle. According to *The Secret Doctrine*, the separation of the poles takes place in a precosmic state which is halfway between the nonbeing of the Absolute and the beginning of the manifested universe. Divine Mind is "the first production of spirit and matter," and is "projected into the phenomenal world as the first aspect of the changeless Absolute."[6] It provides the interface between spirit and matter which is necessary for their integration in the world of form.

Divine Mind is equated with Brahmā, the Creator, the deity of Hindu mythology who brings about the formation of the world. The term *Brahma* derives from a root which means to increase or expand. Thus "as a spider throws out and retracts its web . . . Brahma 'expands' and becomes the Universe woven out of its own substance."[7] Brahma represents that stage of unfoldment in which what lay concealed in the depths of Divine Thought is given definite and objective expression.

H.P.B. states that it is Motion which begets Universal Mind (in Sanskrit *Mahat*), the precursor of manifestation. The world of nature is in constant motion; motion is intrinsic to manifestation. She also states that the movement of Universal Mind is time. Mahat brings form into being, which is a process in time and evokes the potentiality of time. Yet Mahat remains unchanged through all the cycles of worlds it brings into existence. Speaking of the eternal fullness of the Divine Mind, Prem and Ashish refer to the existence at that level of everything in every moment, as was discussed in chapter 9 on time.

> Within [Universal Mind] lies the ever-present simultaneity of all the forms that we experience here as an ordered procession of events. Yet these events are also 'within' Divine Mind. They exist within it, and the time in which we experience them is its time.[8]

Thus the potency of a manifested universe is ever-present within Divine Thought in a kind of eternity, to be played out in the world through time.

Theosophy teaches that nothing can come into being that did not pre-exist in the inner world as ideal plan. All evolves and develops from "the germ of the unknown darkness" according to the order and proportion of the Divine Mind. Prem and Ashish, following H.P.B., compare speech to the objectification of Divine Thought into matter. The inarticulate outflow of divine life is formed into distinct and significant parts, much as we give precise verbal expression to what begins as a vague flow of thought. The word *Logos*, which means 'speech', 'word', or 'reason', is another term signifying the creative, formative aspect of Mahat, the *Word* of Genesis. H.P.B. says:

> Logos (speech, word, verbum) is the rendering in objective expression, as in a photograph, of the concealed thought. The Logos is the mirror reflecting Divine Mind, and the Universe is the mirror of the Logos.[9]

Logos is the Divine Mind in creative operation, the cause of all things, as she says elsewhere.

Geometric Models

According to the Ancient Wisdom, the world issues from Mahat by means of archetypes, the Divine Ideas or Forms of Plato. These are nonmaterial matrices or guiding fields, geometric in nature, which shape forms from within. They are not themselves specific images or patterns of energy but formative principles, ways in which matter can take form, inherent possibilities. Archetypes are reflected in the biological orders, families, genera, species, in the orders of crystals, in the bodily pattern of man. According to Prem and Ashish:

> Whether we think we perceive a clod of earth, a tree, a chair, a man, or even a thought, it is in reality the divine archetypal images of the Universal Mind that we are in fact perceiving or misperceiving . . . . [These] are not so much actual images as formative principles which give rise . . . to images lower down the ladder of being . . . in themselves they are beyond all that we know as form. As the *Upanishads* say, "by the soul must they be seen."[10]

In the theosophical view the concrete forms of our experience are imperfect expressions of these ideal archetypes. They constitute the deeper, generic nature of things, which is only approximated in actuality. Such approximation is evident in crystal formation. If there is ample space and a pure solution of the proper chemicals, crystals will precipitate in perfect form, exactly expressing the geometry of their space lattices. However, such conditions are rare. Crystals have to squeeze into tight places; obstacles get in their way; impurities dissolve in the solution from which they form. They can only approximate the ideal symmetry, though, however deformed, the angle between faces is always exact. Plants, due to their complexity, are even less perfect.

Yet, though never followed exactly, the archetypes serve as blueprints to guide the growing forms. They are like the perfect song on a conceptual level which individual singers bring into being in their unique and often imperfect way. We can glimpse that ideal perfection of the archetypes shining through the facets of crystal, the petal design of a flower, the fluid symmetry of an animal, the form of a lovely woman or well-proportioned man. Through penetrating a natural form such as a rose or crystal in meditation and unifying our consciousness with it, we might come to sense as living reality the exquisite harmony that governs its shape. To the opened eye of the seer all nature is but a symbol, a partial and dim expression of the radiant beauty of the archetypes in the Divine Mind.

Symmetry, Nature's Design

The geometry of the archetypes and the Universal Mind are evident in the principles of symmetry which pervade nature and art. Symmetry shows us a glimpse of the ideal beauty which is reflected in nature, infusing it with order. Symmetry is universal; it can be found everywhere as the broad principle of balance and harmony. It has been familiar to most peoples since the earliest times. Once we become aware of it, we find symmetry all around: in animals, plants, minerals; in textiles, floors, walls; in music, dance, and poetry. As a principle, it applies to the most diverse fields of knowledge. Artists, musicians, choreographers, architects, weavers, printers—physicists, geologists, paleontologists, astronomers, chemists, mathematicians—all these and more find meaning and usefulness in the concept of symmetry. Marjorie Senechal, a mathematician who arranged an interdisciplinary conference on symmetry at Smith College, sees its broad relevance: "In science as well as the arts, symmetry is the geometric plan on which the variations of nature and life are drawn."[11] Principles of symmetry, which means "with measure," can unify large bodies of knowledge.

Mathematics is the natural language of symmetry and its features are expressed in mathematics, group theory for instance. Among the forms of symmetry that can be described mathematically are radial symmetry around a point, as in a daisy; mirror plane symmetry, as in an animal, where left and right sides mirror one another; translation from side to side along a line, as in leaves which appear on a stem at opposite nodes; or screw axis where leaves grow in spiral around the stem. The same patterns of symmetry are repeated over and over in nature and in art. A striking example is the beautiful logarithmic curve that appears in spiral nebulae, in the shell of the chambered nautilus, in the seed pattern on the face of sunflowers, in decorations atop Grecian columns.

Symmetry stands out perhaps most dramatically in crystals. We have all marveled at the delicate patterning of ice crystals in snowflakes with their radial symmetry. The three-

The logarithmic curve is found in many natural forms, such as a spiral galaxy, charged particles in a magnetic field, petal formations.

dimensional symmetry of crystallized minerals is no less striking, as in the eight-sided quartz needle or the four-sided pyramidal points of amethyst. This stark beauty results from internal structure—of atoms in molecules which follow a precise geometrical pattern. For example, common table salt is built of cubes which resemble a three-dimensional checkerboard—"red" cubes filled by sodium atoms and "black" ones by chlorine atoms.

The very foundation of the world of solids as well as the rich variety of substances in the tangible world results from symmetrical patterning of atoms in molecules. The atoms of the chemical elements are organized electromagnetic energy.

The periodic table of elements speaks as eloquently of order as do the systems of crystals. The indeterminacy principle—which states that the path of a particular electron cannot be specified but only the behavior of a large number of them plotted statistically—does not undermine the mathematical properties of order found in chemistry. Even in the complex dance of subatomic matter, particles and their interactions follow laws of symmetry, and physicists have found it a powerful tool in classifying subatomic particles.

Living things, too, show striking examples of harmony and mathematical proportion. The beauty of flowers is based on petal arrangements and flower parts in multiples of three (for monocotyledons) or four or five (for dicotyledons), all patterned geometrically. The lovely pyramidal shape of the spruce results from the correct proportion of the branches to one another. Growing things maintain remarkable order and proportion as their size increases. For example, as the common gourd grows, the rate of growth of its girth at any place remains in constant proportion to the rate of growth of its length, so that its shape is constant as it expands. To achieve this result, the cells must split in various directions, sometimes this way, sometimes that. Though hormones and chemicals are known to be involved in the process, its exact mechanism remains a mystery. Yet it is clear, as D'Arcy Thompson, a biologist who studied proportions in living things, pointed out, the constant motion of growth is not random but follows a consistent pattern.

Living things show a fluid architecture in which the functioning of each part exactly fits the needs of the whole. All levels, from atoms to cells to tissues and organs, are interdependent and coordinated, as vital processes working together. Organisms are self-forming and also goal directed, not random. They show direction and purpose in their activities. F. L. Kunz held that such self-ordering forms operate according to a principle of order, of dynamic geometry: "The self-proportioned geometry of the living orders is the diversified expression of a consistent, universal principle."[12] In theosophical terms, this ordering, mathematical principle is the Divine Mind.

Divine Geometry

Number and mathematical relationships are at the heart of creation according to esoteric philosophy, particularly as expressed in the *Kabbalah* and the Platonic and Pythagorean traditions. The ancient Greeks were imbued with the idea of mathematics as the basis for nature, and they attributed number to a divine source. One, three, and seven are examples of mystic numbers that are fundamental in the unfolding of the universe. They occur in a series of numbers which inevitably unroll from the One as it generates the many. H.P.B. states that "one of the keys to Universal Knowledge is a pure geometrical and numerical system."[13]

For Platonists, this geometrical system was revealed by the Platonic solids. These are geometrical forms which were believed to be the symmetrical, noumenal basis for all form. The ancient idea turned out to be relevant and useful today. These Platonic solids correspond to the space-filling lattices of crystals, such as the cubical pattern of salt, which could be repeated indefinitely to fill all space. There are only fourteen patterns possible for space lattices. Thus, there is corroboration for the ancient belief that these few Platonic solids hold the key to the structure of all nature. Studying these shapes can give insight into geometry as a skeletal principle behind natural forms, the Divine Mind in nature.[14]

Pythagoras, in his theory of the Music of the Spheres, related the concept of number to the vast plan of the cosmos. He saw the universe as constructed according to a musical scale, with everything composed of number and organized according to precise harmonic values. This theory may not be so far-fetched. The Pythagorean concept of harmony has meaning in the context of modern knowledge.

Pythagoras discovered a rational relationship between the length of a string and the note it makes when bowed. For example, if a string is shortened by one half, its note is an octave higher and the number of vibrations doubled. Amazingly, modern mathematicians have discovered that the series of overtones Pythagoras observed is similar to the atomic intervals in crystals, which are also based on whole number ratios.

Harmony in music is related to symmetry in crystals! Pythagoras "heard" mathematics in music; to the eminent mineralogist G. C. Amstutz, the same mathematical relationships became visible in crystals.

> Indeed, the crystals can now literally be seen to be the philosopher's stone, frozen music which presents to the eye, as forms and colors, summaries of the dynamism of molecules, atoms, particles and standing waves . . . .[15]

Platonic and Pythagorean theory, which posits a mathematical basis for the physical world, offers clues as to the outworkings of the archetypes and the Divine Mind.

Mind: Human and Divine

The term *Divine Mind* must have arisen because through the ages people have been struck by the similarity of man's mind and its organizing function to the order found in nature. Art in particular shows the symmetry and design so abundant in natural forms. Mathematicians, too, have faced the dilemma of how it is that the operations of their brains so often describe faithfully the basic order of the universe they perceive. For example, in the mid-1900s the mathematician G.F.B. Riemann playfully invented an internally consistent mathematical system with no parallel lines—for no practical purpose. Later this mathematics turned out to describe aspects of Relativity theory, to fit new findings about nature. Such instances have caused the brain researcher Karl Pribram to wonder whether mind is an expression of some basic ordering principle, that is, whether mental operations reflect the basic order of the universe. He entertains the possibility that "indeed, as proclaimed by all great religious convictions, a unity characterizes this emergent [mind] and the basic order of the universe."[16] He even goes so far as to suggest that "perhaps the very fundamental properties of the universe are therefore mental and not material."[17] This suggestion is reminiscent of Sir James Jeans's idea of the universe as the thought of a mathematical thinker, but one which expresses through our minds as well as through the natural world.

*The Taj Mahal suggests exquisite archetypal perfection
frozen into marble.*

Hermann Weyl, noted for his contributions to mathematics
and to the philosophy of science, also considered the question. He wondered whether the artist copies nature's symmetry or whether the symmetry produced in art comes from
the same source as that in nature. He concluded that symmetry in art is not necessarily copied from nature but rather
results from the quality of the artist's mind. The laws of harmony found in nature also appear in man's mind; both
emerge from a common source:

> I am inclined to think with Plato that the mathematical idea
> is the common origin of both [the artist's mind and natural
> symmetry]: the mathematical laws governing nature are the
> origin of symmetry in nature, and the intuitive realization
> of the idea in the creative artist's mind its origin in art.[18]

Esoteric philosophy holds that both man and the universe
are products of the creative, nonmaterial background: their
characteristics reflect the orderly nature of That. H.P.B. explains that man's mind, Manas, is the vehicle of Divine Ideation, "a direct ray from the Universal Mahat." She sees Manas
as being "only Mahat individualized, as the sun's rays are in-

dividualized in bodies that absorb them."[19] The Divine Mind reveals its own nature in the human abilities to conceptualize, to see relationships and patterns in diversity, to produce pattern and design in art, mathematics, science, and to organize experience into meaningful, interrelated wholes. The great insights that have inspired mathematics, science, and philosophy, as well as the eternal beauty of great art, dramatically reveal the creative potential of the Divine Mind. But so, too, do our more humble everyday uses of mental faculties. We have a powerful inner urge toward order, toward perceiving harmonies and relationships, which we use everyday.

Yet, as we know all too well, the inner tendency toward order can become eclipsed, so that we sometimes feel confused and disorganized. The disorganization occurs in the octave of our mind and emotions that tends to be split off from our deeper selves. Ironically, this seeming estrangement is the result of an aspect of the Divine Mind itself.

The Secret Doctrine states that the Divine Mind is a manifestation of the subjective, inward pole of being—consciousness. Prem and Ashish refer to it as "the flame of living consciousness that burns in the core of all existent being." Just as we in our innermost selves experience our own thoughts and bodies as objective, so, as H.P.B. says, "Divine Mind is the Subject which experiences simultaneously the total being of the universe existing in time."[20] Its subjectivity is diffused throughout the cosmos. Mahat not only "constitutes the Basis of the Subjective side of manifested being," but it is also "the source of all manifestation of individual consciousness."[21] Thus when we feel "I am I," that essential consciousness of ourselves as individuals, we are experiencing an aspect of universal cognition or Divine Mind.

Unfortunately, this basic sense of self (*Ahamkara* in Sanskrit) too often assumes the form of egotism in us, which throws a veil between our awareness and Divine Mind. Rather than pure self-consciousness which radiates from and is connected to Divine Mind, we tend to feel self-defensive isolation with the need to hang onto and build up ourselves as separated egos. We feel that our separate identity is precious, a basic necessity. This is a perversion of divine Thought,

"dark Egoism, the progeny of Mahat on the lower plane."[22]
We trap ourselves in the prison of egotism and disorder and
lose sight of our deeper aspects.

Order in Our Lives

Though perhaps we can see principles of organization more
easily in nature than in human affairs, theosophy proclaims
that order from a divine source is also at work in our lives.
Often we cannot trace orderly sequences in what befalls us,
and our lives seem capricious, unpredictable, chancy. We
feel, as Loren Eiseley expressed it, that "order strives against
the unmitigated chaos lurking along the convulsive backbone
of the world."[23]

Yet all the while the Divine Mind underlies our being. We
are at all times linked to Universal Mind, an ever-present,
lawful background, which supports us and gives us life from
within. In this superconscious realm lies an orderly pattern
that affects us at all levels and reflects in our lives. As this
orderliness impresses itself on nature, it also presses toward
harmony within us.

We can learn to use this potential more fully and apply
it in practical situations, as well as in intellectual and artistic
endeavors. When we feel disorganized and pulled apart, we
can call on this deeper strata of mind reflected in us from the
Divine Mind. If through contemplation we arrive at a solid
conviction that the world stems from Divine Mind and is
basically lawful, what seemed chaotic may appear as part of a
harmonious pattern that can be detected from a long-range
view. We can come to realize that the disorder in human affairs comes from disorder and disharmony within each of us
and between us, not from nature (chapter 13). Even though
sometimes chaos and violence seem to dominate in the
foreground, always in the background there is system and
harmony. As Prem and Ashish put it, "beneath the chaotic
movements of events [are] the eternal patterns of the cosmic
harmony."[24]

One way to begin the process of increasing inner order is to
notice the symmetry all around, in natural forms, in art, ar-

chitecture, music, even wallpaper and textiles. As our minds become saturated with the idea of symmetry, we can pass to a deeper concept of order. We might sense all nature as a moving order, as in music where all the rhythms and tones are harmonized, all the parts held together in a dynamic structure. We might even glimpse the reality of pure order as a principle not dependent on objects. This awareness can reestablish inner order and regenerate and renew us. As crystals precipitate from a nucleus within a chaos of moving molecules in the mother solution, we can create an inner nucleus of order that will continue to grow as it draws on an amorphous mass of experience. Our outer, worldly selves can become charged with order and beauty, even as the deeper levels of the higher mind are charged with the order of Divine Mind. Though we too seldom touch this reality in our depths, we are carriers of divine order, which we can learn to project within ourselves and out into the world.

11

Sevenfold Illusion

> There is one reality but this reality has multiple
> dimensions, multiple levels, and multiple aspects.
> Physicists and mystics deal with different aspects of
> reality.
>
> David Bohm

Only in very recent times have we considered the visible,
tangible world as the sole reality. Since the beginning of
human thought, peoples have believed themselves to be surrounded by invisible realms. Even today tribal peoples hold
ceremonies and rituals to contact the unseen. In ancient Egypt
and in the Mystery Schools everywhere and at all times, the
importance of invisible realms and beings has been acknowledged in sacred rituals. The world's religions still acknowledge such intangibles with their ceremonies in which they
seek to contact something beyond the physical world.

Modern science, based on Cartesian dualism with its
"hard" materiality, has produced a climate that is not fa-
vorable to acceptance of the supersensible. In this view the
physical world is the real world. This belief, which has
prevailed in the West for some 200 years, led to the
materialistic values so prevalent in modern times. Yet the
very science which sprang from materialistic philosophy

points to realms all around us that are not available to our senses, realms that we contact through technology rather than ritual. No one has ever seen electricity, yet our cities at night are ablaze with its visible effects. Our television sets and radios make unseen energies visible and audible. X-rays and ultrasound precipitate the interior areas of our bodies into visible images. Science has taught us to use energies which we will never see or feel directly. Through technology today the invisible and unseen enter into and affect our world of the senses, much as the ancients were connected with the unseen worlds through ritual.

Scientists now recognize the validity of realities that we will never experience directly—from subatomic particles to galaxies detectable only by the radio waves they emit. Our senses can respond to only a limited range of frequencies. Bees see ultraviolet light and snakes respond to infrared, frequencies which are imperceptible to us. Ultrasound is real sound,

Even material as dense as brass appears less than solid under the microscope.

though not within the range our ears can sense. X-rays, cosmic rays, radio waves, microwaves constantly travel undetected through the space around us. If we could perceive all the supersensible influences in our immediate surroundings, we would be bombarded by intensely energetic movement, a "buzzing, booming confusion" far less comprehensible than the newborn's strange new world is to him or her. Physicist Henry Margenau holds that in science "we simply cannot have only one set of principles about how reality works. We need to allow for a number of alternate realities."[1]

Seven Levels of Being

Theosophy allows for "alternate realities" in the form of superphysical spheres which interpenetrate the physical world. Between the ultimate noumenal unity and the solidity and diversity of the physical world there are intermediate states or fields. These range from the filmiest supersensual realms close to the nonmaterial all the way to the density and definiteness of the physical. As electromagnetic energy forms a spectrum from high-energy, extremely short X-rays to low-energy mile-long radio waves, these fields described in eso teric philosophy form a spectrum that extends from the finest to the densest, from the most energetic and powerful to the comparative inertia of the physical world.

According to theosophy there are seven levels and each is characterized by its own unique state of rarefied matter, with all but the physical too fine for our senses to register. We might imagine the sevenfold world as a series of interpenetrating concentric spheres, each composed of its unique kind of supersensuous stuff. These seven realms were known to the ancients and given various names at different times. They can be correlated with yoga philosophy, the religion of ancient Egypt, the Kabbalistic system, the skandhas of Buddhism, and many other traditions.

Much of modern theosophical literature written in the late 19th and the early 20th centuries came out before field theory was known. The early writers referred to these realms as *planes*. This term is useful, but it implies a two-dimensional, layercake concept rather than interpenetration, which *fields* conveys. In order to make connections with the traditional literature, I will use the two terms interchangeably, though *field* is a more accurate and modern term.

In modern theosophical parlance, the planes can be designated as the physical, emotional, mental, intuitional, spiritual will, plus two more spiritual levels hard to characterize in human terms. They are named for human functions because not only do they exist throughout nature but they also comprise the various levels of man's being. The most obvious level of this sevenfold scheme is the familiar physical world of solids, liquids, and gases that our senses register all around us, the world of nature and of things. Interpenetrating the visible physical plane is a level called *etheric* in some of the literature, which consists of superphysical states finer than gases but still close to the physical level. It is a high-energy realm, closely associated with prana or universal energy, that infuses vitality into physical organisms. The etheric level shades into the "astral" or emotional field, which is said to be very fluid and flowing and brilliant with psychedelic colors. This realm is marked by all shades of surging, longing, cringing, or aggressive feelings, as well as elevated emotions like esthetic appreciation and devotion. Next comes the field of Manas or the mind, even more subtle and rarefied than the astral field, and characterized by a more stable, orderly quality. There are two aspects to this field, one of which gravitates toward the astral and physical worlds and the other toward the more spiritual realms. From this field come meaning and significance, and it reflects the order of the Divine Mind that is found everywhere in nature. The next field of Buddhi or intuition is numinous and radiant. It lies close to the One, and its outstanding characteristic is unity. The level of Atma is the most rarefied, essentially one with the noumenal Reality.

Each of us has our own localization in all of the seven levels. Thus we are composed of interpenetrating fields which blend together in us. H.P.B. refers to man as "a total, a compound unit of Matter and Spirit, which together act on seven planes of being and consciousness."[2]

Though all the fields pervade all of nature, we can see the special characteristic of each most easily by introspection. We can readily sense the stable, solid quality of our physical bodies, dominated by gravity, so that they stay in place and show the massy, weighty quality that is characteristic of the physical world. Physical stability contrasts to the labile, changeable quality of the emotions with their dynamic energy. The ancients called this latter realm the Water Element, and water is an apt symbol for its fluidity, both in us and in the emotional (or astral) sphere of nature. The etheric links the physical and emotional levels, so that physical reactions accompany emotional states.

We can see in ourselves how emotions differ from logical thinking, with its step-by-step orderly processes. Thinking is structured, ordering, organized, not diffuse or with sudden flare-ups, as are emotions. Thought is a function of mind (Manas). By contrast, the intuition in the theosophical sense (Buddhi) does give sudden illuminations. These are always unitive if they are genuine intuitions. They might bring diverse elements together into a synthesis or reveal unexpected relationships. The intuitional realm is also the source of inspiration and of many mystical states and expansions of consciousness. It reflects the unity of the One in various ways.

The spiritual will (Atma) is the One itself turned toward the manifest world, so to speak. In us it is the very sense of self, of being an individual, yet at the same time being one with the All. Atma is like a point of light in an ocean of light—greater than the great, smaller than the small.

The rainbow can symbolize the spectrum formed by these different levels. The unique quality of each level compares to the distinct colors, each with its special beauty, with all necessary for full expression. As white light breaks into the colors of the rainbow, so the One Life breaks into the qualities of the seven planes. Their orderly structure reveals the Divine Mind, with its noumenal order. As Prem and Ashish see it, "The seven levels are the very structure of the cosmos, the very bed-plate on which it is built."[3]

The image of the rainbow is imperfect because the various levels are not really separate and distinct bands with only a little overlap. It is convenient to study the planes separately, but they are never isolated from one another, as the systems of the body can be studied separately though they do not function apart from one another. The seven fields are mutually penetrating forms of energy—from the finest to the visible, physical world—which constantly interact. All the levels occupy the same space and all the subtler levels have impact on the physical plane. We can see an analogy to the interpenetration of the planes in a bar magnet which is surrounded by, and subject to, both the gravitational field (it can fall) and the electromagnetic field (which results in its attraction and repulsion).

We can experience the interaction of various fields in ourselves. Our every thought is tinged by some degree of emotion, and all feelings have some accompanying thought. Both thought and feeling affect the body and its physiology. This happens when we blush or tremble from fright, or rush into action on an impulse. Psychosomatic medicine has also clearly demonstrated this relation.

All seven strands are inextricably interwoven in nature and in us. They are the raw material from which nature's forms are fashioned, all the levels intermingled into a single whole, the seven-colored palette from which the shades and tints of life are taken. The many levels of reality intermix to form the whole we know as nature.

Evidence for Unseen Energies

The world view of modern physics is much more compatible with the idea of superphysical realities than was 19th-century mechanism and materialism. Einstein showed that matter can be converted into energy. Since there are many kinds and degrees of energy and states of matter, the esoteric doctrine of various fine states of matter and energy is plausible. Thus physics opened the door to the possibility of imperceptible realms, as it showed the reality of frequencies beyond human perception.

There are experimental data from parapsychology that violate a materialistic world picture and suggest energies and fields so far unknown to science. For example, a noted healer, under strictest double-blind conditions, "treated" bottles of water by holding them between his hands. Plants watered from these bottles grew significantly better than did controls. The experimenter, Bernard Grad of McGill University, could find no other explanation than that an unknown energy entered the water through the healer.[4] Another example of unknown energy is found in experiments with psychokinesis (PK), the ability to affect matter through nonphysical means. In one experiment children gifted in PK were able to bend straight aluminum bars into an S shape without touching them, even though the bars were sealed in transparent tubes.[5] Force fields detected around living things are also under investigation. Burr and Ravitz discovered such fields, which they called the fields of life or L-fields. Electrical readings taken on various living creatures revealed interesting information. From such readings it was possible to forecast the productivity of cotton seeds. Trees showed daily, monthly, and seasonal rhythms of electrical fluctuations which were not related to temperature, dampness, or barometric pressure. Humans showed two-week periodical fluctuations, a finding that was substantiated by 50,000 readings on 500 subjects.[6] Kirlian photography also reveals electrical fields connected with changes in living things.

Biologists working in the framework of holistic philosophy have extended the concept of L-fields to "morphogenetic fields," which help account for the apparent guiding influence that shapes living organisms as they grow. These fields are believed to mold developing cells, tissues, and organisms. For example, a heart forming in an embryo would be molded by a field with a heart-like structure. Plant physiologist Rupert Sheldrake has extended the idea of morphogenetic fields to account for the "hundredth monkey phenomenon."[7] There is evidence that some monkeys on an island near Japan started to wash gritty, freshly dug potatoes, and that shortly this behavior spread to all the monkeys on the island. Curiously, monkeys on nearby islands, with no physical contact with the potato-washers, also took up the habit. Sheldrake hypothesizes a field by means of which communication can occur within a species over distance and even at future times. This transmission process is thought to occur according to the principle of resonance, as when a note struck on a piano evokes response from octaves above and below itself. The hypothesis of morphogenetic fields helps explain many mysteries in embryology and in the growth of plants and animals, in animal behavior, and even in ESP

William Tiller, a renowned crystallographer at Stanford, after studying the data on ESP and L-fields, concluded that "we seem to be dealing with new energy fields completely different from those known to us via conventional science."[8] He acknowledges that some experimental procedures in parapsychology are questionable because it is hard to get a "clean" experiment in some cases: "However, the body of experimental data of this type is so vast and growing so rapidly that it cannot be denied much longer."[9] Following yoga philosophy (which coincides with the theosophical view of man), he postulates seven principles operating in man, each with its own type of substance and each obeying one of seven unique sets of natural laws. These substances, he presumes, are everywhere in nature and interpenetrate the human body. Dr. Tiller concludes that "the universe seems to organize and radiate information in other dimensions than just the physical space-time frame."[10] The evidence also led him to conclude that "at some level we are all interconnected to each other and to all things on this planet."[11]

Tiller is in the forefront of science, which has opened to these mysteries only a little way. Even modern parapsychology has but scratched the surface of the unseen worlds taught in esoteric philosophy, which has enormous depths not imagined by any modern researcher unfamiliar with it. Scientists like Dr. Tiller who dare to explore ancient traditions for their bearing on modern findings may unveil more and more of nature's hidden realms. Perhaps the time will come when scientists and seers, rather than being concerned with separate spheres, will investigate the same aspects of reality and come to a shared vision.

The Seven and the One

According to theosophy, the matter of the seven planes congeals from the background reality of the One. We may think of the levels emerging from the unmanifested, each in turn giving rise to the succeeding level of density, much as invisible water vapor can become clouds, then water, then ice. Through stages the inchoate, luminous One unfolds its potentiality in increasing definiteness and density. The unbroken radiant light condenses and crystallizes by degrees into a myriad of distinct forms.

In one sense the subtler, finer fields or planes are closer to the One, more "spiritual." Yet at the same time Atma or the One at the highest level of manifestation is forcefully present at every level. It is both the highest rung of the ladder and the entire ladder itself. Like electricity, Atma is everywhere, though mostly unobservable. We cannot see electricity in electrons, in brain waves, in the electrical discharges of living things. Atma, too, is in every atom of the universe and pervades all nature, all levels. Even more, it is the animating power of all that is, the bedrock reality behind all forms, the inner life of all manifestation. All the planes are but differentiations of the one Reality on which they rest. As H.P.B. said:

> [Atman] is in every atom of the universe, the six principles in nature being all the outcome—the variously differentiated aspects—of the Seventh and One, the only Reality in the universe.[12]

But even the seventh principle from which the others emerge "is but a temporary and periodic ray of the One eternal and infinite Flame of Fire."[13] H.P.B. sees the world of manifestation as "a film for creative and formative purposes" which "manifests in seven states."[14] Matter in all its states is the vehicle which responds to the creative impulses of the Divine Mind. As described by Dr. I. K. Taimni the universe is but the outer manifestation of a great spiritual consciousness which has the innate power to diversify its pure, homogeneous energy at many levels of subtlety and ultimately to project material form.

The Illusory World

The rainbow symbolizes the planes of nature for a reason other than its orderly bands of color: its evanescence and il-

lusory quality are like the manifest world as it stands in relation to the abiding One. The rainbow is the short-lived effect
of white light being refracted by water droplets. On a much
larger scale, all that exists throughout the cosmos is but the
temporary, ephemeral effect of the One Life refracted through
the screen of objectivity. According to *The Secret Doctrine:*

> The universe is called, with everything in it, Maya
> [illusion], because all is temporary therein, from the
> ephemeral life of a firefly to that of the Sun. Compared to
> the eternal immutability of the One, and the changelessness
> of that Principle, the Universe, with its evanescent ever-
> changing forms, must be necessarily . . . no better than a
> will-o'-the-wisp.[15]

Prem and Ashish explain how the Absolute Reality is
obscured by the birth of the manifest world: "The Above, or
unmanifest principles, are 'shut out', while the Below, or
manifest principles, are left as the Great Illusion, the magic
play or Maya."[16]

We know that the visible world is made up of molecules
which consist of aggregates of atoms, and that atoms result
from standing waves in nonmaterial force fields. We cannot
directly sense these fields which underly all physical objects.
Our perception is limited to an aspect, a partial revelation of
the underlying reality. The world of the senses is incomplete,
illusory because it is based on that which is unavailable to our
senses. Theosophy teaches that, similarly, we see only partial
aspects in the manifest world, not the totality. We cannot
catch the reality of things in the moment when they "pass like
a flash through the material world," where our senses record
only certain aspects of material existence, as H.P.B. says. We
see them torn out of their organic, supersensible connections
and deprived of their universal relationships. We can comprehend only a degree of reality, that which is illusory and
impermanent. Therefore, as the *Immutable Sutra* says:

> The phenomena of life may be likened unto a dream, a
> bubble, a shadow, the glistening dew, or lightning flash;
> and thus they ought to be contemplated.

Yet the world which we see only partially is real enough to
us while we are in it. We have to conform to its partial reality

in our daily lives, in our physical situation. For instance, we cannot drive in traffic without acute awareness of physical reality. But we become so engrossed in the illusion that we lose sight of a fuller reality behind it, as when in a dream we do not realize we are dreaming. Sometimes we catch a glint of the light from beyond; an intuitive flash gives a hint of something behind the "perishing particulars." We may glimpse the insubstantiality of our lives, as Walt Whitman indicates in his poem "Appearances":

> Sometimes how strange and clear to the soul,
>   That all these solid things are indeed but apparitions,
>   concepts, non-realities.

One important aspect of spiritual growth lies in cultivating a larger, more complete view, of developing an underlying attitude that goes beyond surface appearances. Along the way to attaining this, we may come to realize for ourselves that each of us is made up of seven principles which are inherent in the seven cosmic principles, just as our bodies are composed of the same matter that comprises all the physical cosmos. We are connected with the universe at every level, and therefore we have a far richer potential than we have begun to express. As H.P.B. pointed out, "Each of [man's] seven principles is an heir in full to, and partaker of, the seven principles of the 'Great Mother,' [the universal life of all]."[17]

Meditation and yoga practices show us how to begin to activate dormant layers of our consciousness, to awake to a wider spectrum of being, a more comprehensive view. As Ravi Ravindra, a professor of both physics and religion, has said: ". . . yoga is that teaching by which the unhearable becomes heard and the unseen becomes seen . . . . One becomes available to an altogether different, subtler and more comprehensive order of reality."[18] As we begin to actualize the seven principles in ourselves more and more and understand their relation to the One, we will discover all the rainbow's seven colors in and around us and also the white light from which they arise.

12

Progressive Development

> The Secret Doctrine teaches the progressive develop-
> ment of everything, worlds as well as atoms; and this
> stupendous development has neither conceivable
> beginning nor imaginable end.
>
> H. P. Blavatsky, *The Secret Doctrine*

*E*volution does not pertain only to early-earth volcanoes, dinosaurs, and primates of the distant past—an ancient history completely removed from our daily lives. It is a living principle at work within us now. Whenever we effortlessly move a hand to grasp, to build, to write, or to caress, we are making use of an ability that took millennia to develop. When we unconsciously focus our eyes for close work or look into the distance with depth perception, or when we sort and categorize or think logically, we are indebted to intricate sequences of development that began in the distant past. As we use the amazing abilities shared by highly evolved organisms, we seldom think of the eons of evolution behind them, or recognize that the whole evolutionary sequence is present in us now, or that latent in the depths of our unconscious lies the seed of all future capacities that we and our species will develop. To understand evolution is to understand ourselves.

The Secret Doctrine depicts evolution on the grand scale, cosmic and spiritual as well as physical. It views the non-material background Reality as the creative fount from which life's many streams emerge. Our finite world developed "from within without," the end result of slow and gradual emanation from the infinite source—the Divine Mind. Thus, theosophy parts with science in its account of the rich and variegated display of living forms which evolution has produced. Whereas scientists look mostly to matter for the origin of life, according to theosophy unseen noumenal forces shape the varying forms as they come and go, adhering to a hidden design. The transcendent Source continually sustains and supports all being, as it holds all parts together in dynamic relationship with the whole.

Theosophy asserts that the impetus for the evolution of forms comes from the urge to release the potential of consciousness, not, as scientists believe, fortuitous changes on the material side. Science, which can study only the history of forms, cannot glimpse the power of consciousness in the background, working through the Divine Mind to create forms suitable for its embodiment at different phases. H.P.B. made it clear that "all things had their origin in Spirit—evolution having originally begun from above and proceeding downwards . . . ."[1] Form is but the expression of consciousness at a particular level of unfoldment. Consciousness in the guise of the Divine Mind, the subjective side of nature, is the driving force behind evolution.

All the basic metaphysical principles are involved and come into play in this phenomenon of evolution: unity, time, space, motion, polarity, fields and planes, cycles. Each principle is activated and comes alive in the ever-changing world as it evolves to express more and more of the divine potential. Space and time, or the space-time of relativity theory, are the stage on which the drama of evolution unfolds. But it is a strange, living stage in which the actors are of the stuff of the stage itself, somewhat as in a motion picture the images are at base no different from the screen. Time arises with the first thrill of life that awakens within the depths of Dark Space.

In that moment the whole stupendous evolutionary cycle begins, perhaps somewhat as modern cosmologists describe as the "Big Bang." Motion and change set going an endless chain of being which puts forth ever more complex links, on and on into unimaginable stretches of time. At last the whole enormous scheme is drawn back once more into a pralaya or night of Dark Space, when once more "Time was not for it lay asleep in the Infinite Bosom of Duration."[2] Till then the time and Bright Space of a living universe will support evolution as it develops ever more sensitive forms.

The Enhancement of Consciousness

H.P.B. emphasized that evolution is *caused*, and is far from being a random sequence, as many scientists still hold. She clearly indicates that evolution has direction: "The whole order of nature evinces a progressive march towards a higher life."[3] The whole vast evolutionary scheme releases the powers of consciousness—through the most elementary sensitivities of the plant and even mineral kingdoms to superhuman intelligence yet to be unfolded. Forms such as the human form with its unimaginably complex brain can function with new orders of intelligence that are far beyond that of earlier simple forms. Evolution moves forward to produce ever more sensitive forms, through which greater degrees of consciousness and ever higher reaches of the Divine Mind can manifest.

The direction of evolution becomes obvious when we look at the kingdoms of nature. As Teilhard de Chardin showed, the drive is toward the "complexification" of form accompanied by enhancement of consciousness. As forms become more complex, the conscious life, the "within of things" in Teilhard's words, becomes richer, more subtle, more varied. Even at the most fundamental material level, rocks react to immense heat and pressure deep within the earth, to the slow pressure of running water, to the disintegrating effect of plant life. Although Teilhard agrees with theosophy that even here there is a dim consciousness, the inner life of minerals must be faint and diffuse. Plants reach toward the sun with their

The spiral is a universal symbol for evolution.

leaves as their roots tunnel into the earth. They respond to music and even to human communication. Animals, from worms to chimpanzees, feel some degree of pain and pleasure, whether from the slight burning of an acidic environment or as demonstrated by the playful antics of the young. Along with the intricacies of the human body, evolution has given man sensitivities and capacities such as for mathematics and art which could never be predicted from our closest animal kin. Life is continually developing organisms which are more and more responsive to the inner demands of consciousness. Evolution marches forward with increasingly complex forms, which express an ever richer inner life.

Science and theosophy both recognize that, in spite of the diversity of forms, evolution attests to the oneness of life. Evolutionists agree that all living things share a past lost in the mists of time, from which they arose from the most archaic one-celled forms of life. Plants, animals, and microorganisms share a universal language with man—the code by which their DNA communicates its directives. All living things grow as wholes and organize themselves toward the shared goal of expressing more perfectly the features and functions which inhere in them. All of this takes place in a milieu that is dependent upon the prior evolution of our galaxy, our sun, the earth, and the chemical elements, which were all essential for the delicate balance of chemistry, temperature, and other factors necessary for life to arise. All living things thus have their roots not only in the Earth, but in the universe itself. They all inhere in the One.

The Chance Hypothesis

A growing number of scientists are coming to believe, as do theosophists, that all the conditions necessary for life to arise could not have come about at the same time just by chance. Sir Frederick Gowland Hopkins, who first discovered certain amino acids needed in human nutrition, described the origin of life as "the most improbable and the most significant event in the history of the universe." In recent decades amino acids, the complex building blocks of proteins, sprang into being in the laboratory under simulated early earth conditions, and fragments of DNA and sugars vital to life have been synthesized. But mystery still shrouds the way the many complex factors necessary for life combined in nature to form living organisms. H. Quastler, a biochemist, is one among many scientists and mathematicians who have tried to calculate the odds against the coincidence of all the many factors necessary for life. His figure is 10^{-301}—an unimaginably remote chance that life could have arisen just by accident.[4] Some feel that the immensity of the earth's age makes the chance hypothesis more likely, but mathematicians working out the odds do not find it so.

Complexification

Though science has pushed the explanation of life back farther and farther, it has not answered the fundamental questions about the drive toward ever more highly developed and sensitive living forms. "Survival of the fittest" cannot explain why life should have progressed beyond one-celled organisms, which are eminently fit and still survive today. Living things "run uphill," as it were, to ever greater order rather than following the Second Law of Thermodynamics, which predicts "thermal death" through maximum entropy as heat and energy disperse equally through space. What governs this impulse and striving? Is there a principle within the life process itself that impels the struggle for self-fulfillment? How could living creatures result from chance?

Albert Szent-Gyorgy, a Nobel laureate in biochemistry, suggested that the drive toward greater and more complex order may be a fundamental principle of nature. Ilya Prigogine, a Belgian physical chemist, took the explanation further. He won the Nobel prize for his mathematical formulas which explain how greater complexity arises. He demonstrated mathematically that when open systems like seeds or ova or any living creature (dissipative structures in his words) reach a certain complexity, they tend to fall apart. The energy that holds together their cells, subatomic particles, and other levels of organization is bonded less stably in complex systems. However, the parts, rather than just dispersing, tend to reorganize themselves into a new whole, but at a higher level of complexity. It is as though a complicated tinker toy falls apart from its own weight. But rather than lying in a heap, the parts reassemble themselves into an even more complex form.

The implications of this surprising discovery are only beginning to be worked out, but it seems to be a new piece to fit into the puzzle of evolution. This concept fits in very well with the theosophical view. It suggests specifically how evolution is impelled by inner intelligence or consciousness, the Divine Mind, to develop more complex forms to express ever-increasing degrees of consciousness. It helps explain how, in spite of the many imperfections and dead ends in evolution, life continues to evolve into ever higher orders of intelligence.

Types and Archetypes

The great variety of forms result, as H.P.B. explains, because evolution systematically reveals the divine archetypes, the Ideas of Plato. Forms unfold through evolution according to the pattern impressed on them by the archetype that governs their particular structure. There are distinct types, families, and genera because different groups are shaped by different nonmaterial structural patterns or archetypes. Gaps in the fossil record would be predicted by this view, as different types of forms are governed by different archetypal patterns.[5]

Evidence bears this out. The forward motion of evolution is not always gradual. The difference in conscious life between minerals, plants, animals, and humans is not just a matter of degree, but rather a transformation, a quantum leap into another order of being. The biologist Theodosius Dobzhansky called each such leap a "new transcendence." Glaring gaps also appear between non-nucleated cells and those with a nucleus, nonvertebrates and vertebrates, reptiles and birds, sea life and land forms. Conventional neo-Darwinian theory, which posits steady, progressive change from the simple to the complex, cannot explain the many outstanding gaps in the fossil record.

D'Arcy Thompson, a zoologist and mathematician, posited a "principle of discontinuity" for which he found evidence among organic as well as inorganic forms. He studied Pythagoras and, like a Greek geometrician, saw in nature traces of the abstract forms of an ideal world. The hexagons of the beehive and the turtle's shell, the ram's horn, the path of a moth all embody mathematical perfection. Through mathematical analysis of forms, Thompson found that "good" form often shows simple, numerical regularity. He showed that shapes and structures of various related animals express variations of a constant, mathematically defined form. Recently this insight was tested by drawing figures on a computer. The basic form of a coiled shell can be changed from the shape of a nautilus to that of a clam to that of a snail by changing simple gradients such as the rate of growth in one direction.

Thompson was convinced that different geometric configurations define various types in nature. The forms within a type can be transformed into one another, but the different types based on different geometry stand distinct and cannot be converted into one another. He claimed: "A 'principle of discontinuity,' then, is inherent in all our classifications, whether mathematical, physical, or biological . . . . Nature proceeds from one type to another . . . to seek for stepping-stones across the gaps between is to seek in vain forever."[6]

In his theory of "punctuated equilibria," the biologist Stephan Gould provides a mechanism which would account for some of the gaps in evolution. He believes that change can occur in a brief, intense spurt between stable states when a subpopulation migrates and becomes isolated. Under such conditions genetic change can proceed much more quickly than in a large population.[7] This view of evolution coincides with some esoteric teachings, which describe such segregation as the means by which new human types are evolved. It does not necessarily conflict with the concept of archetypes guiding the development of forms from within but rather provides a clue as to one method in which the potentials of the Divine Mind are further released.

Through his mathematical analysis of living forms, D'Arcy Thompson took a major stride in biology toward the theosophical position. He perceived that changes in form are due less to pressures from the external environment than to the unfolding of an "internal" plan or archetype, for as H.P.B. says, "the Universe is worked and guided from within outward."[8]

Pre-adaptations are another of evolution's mysteries for which current theory has no satisfactory answer. Why should certain reptiles start developing "useless" bony structures that only much later evolve into the wings of birds? Why should the fins of certain fish destined never to leave the water change to a system of bones which later would support their descendants on land? It looks as though "useless" features like these arose for the sake of future developments, or in theosophical terms, the unfoldment of further potentiality of the archetypes.

As we have seen, many biologists now agree that living things have within them a basic drive towards higher forms of organization. Many regard the potential for higher forms of life as residing in the first cell that arose, or even in matter itself. *The Secret Doctrine* asserts that every atom and particle is imbued with Divine Mind, which energizes it to move to higher levels of organization, that the whole of the divine potentiality is inherent everywhere; through evolution it slowly unfolds. The exquisite order of Divine Mind and its archetypes continually presses downward and outward to reveal itself more fully in ever more complex forms.

According to theosophy, the embodiment of the archetypes is not a mechanical process in which a blueprint is exactly duplicated. The archetypes are rather motifs or themes which are subject to infinite variations. Butterflies, for instance, can be found in seemingly numberless colors and shapes, showing the creative richness of the archetype they express. Even today new species of various kinds of creatures are turning up all over the world. It seems the Divine Mind uses forms as a painter uses his canvas—to embody the rich imaginative potential of mind. As Von Bertalanffy put it, evolution "seems a cornucopia of *evolution creatrice,* a drama full of suspense . . . ."

Involution and Evolution

Evolution unfolds the divine potential through orderly cycles and stages of development. The principle of cycles is intermingled with evolution at every point. The archetypes precipitate as ever more complex forms in the material world in accordance with the cyclic development of consciousness, as the great geologic ages in part reveal. The sequential unfolding of the archetype's potential from simple to complex proceeds cyclically, according to an inner order—in "the Divine thought . . . lies concealed the plan of every future Cosmogony."[9]

Along with cycles of the evolution of form which can be studied by scientists, theosophy points to a previous cycle of involution in which consciousness becomes more and more deeply involved in matter; there is "double evolution in two contrary directions."[10] H.P.B. speaks of the "interaction of two principles in nature, the inner Conscious Principle adapting itself to physical nature and the innate potentialities of the latter."[11] Through this double process consciousness gradually becomes concretized and matter spiritualized. In the first phase pure consciousness, the "spirit" aspect of the two primordial poles, "plunges deeper and deeper into materiality."[12] On the material side of this phase, the planes of nature are built by degrees, from subtle to concrete, until the dense physical world finally appears through "a gradual materialization of forms until a fixed ultimate . . . is reached."[13] The entire scheme lasts for eons and eons and unfolds according to cosmic design. The movement is from the formless, inchoate, homogeneous to the differentiated and materialized. Consciousness becomes more and more defined, limited, sharp, focused as it infuses ever more complex forms.

At the mid-point of the cycle, the direction changes and the movement arches upward. Forms gradually become more refined and etherialized, and consciousness is released bit by bit from imprisonment in separative forms to its primal state of undifferentiated unity. "On the descending arc it is the spiritual which gradually transforms into the material. On the middle line of the base, spirit and matter are equilibrized in Man. On the ascending arc spirit is slowly reasserting itself at the expense of the physical or Matter."[14] At the end of the cycle all is drawn back into a homogeneous state of unimpeded oneness—"perpetual, ever-ceasing evolution circles back in its incessant progress through eons of duration into its original status—Absolute Unity."[15]

The Secret Doctrine sketches many stages in the vast scheme and designates these as Chains, Rounds, Races. Each cycle and subcycle has its phase of involution in which it moves from superphysical fields into the physical and then evolves back into superphysical realms. H.P.B. describes unimaginably long time spans in which waves of life produced mineral, vegetable, and animal forms that were predecessors of the ones we know. She paints a picture of man evolving in superphysical realms at the same time that the physical world was developing and solidifying. The Secret Doctrine postulates "the birth of the astral [man] before the physical, the former being a model for the latter."[16] Finally, the human consciousness inhabits a physical body, still on the arc of involution, with consciousness not yet firmly implanted. Human beings continue to evolve on all levels, spiritual, intellectual, emotional, and physical. The biologist Erich Jantsch perceived that man lives on more levels than earlier forms of life. "We contain the entire evolution within us, but it is orchestrated to a fuller and richer extent than in less complex forms of life."[17]

All that has ever gone into making our earth is buried somewhere in our present. Time moves forward bearing with it all that has gone before. As the old man carries his past within himself and is the present witness and outcome of all he ever was, so the world with its numberless forms, peoples, cultures has risen phoenix like from the ashes of the past. The world today and each of us who share in it are in a sense living history.

Man, the Centerpiece of Evolution

H.P.B. makes the startling statement that "all in nature tends to become man"[18]—that all nature tends toward evolving the human potential. She also holds that man is "the masterpiece of evolution." She views humans as the repository of divinity, the integration of spirit and matter for which evolution is drawn forward. "Every form on earth, every speck (atom) in Space strives in its efforts toward self-formation to follow the model placed for it in the 'Heavenly Man' . . . . Man is the highest physical and ultimate form on this earth . . . the culmination of the divine incarnations on Earth."[19] Although he is not yet finished, man clearly indicates the direction of evolution toward unfoldment of higher and higher reaches of consciousness and mind.

In the middle of the entire scheme, an equilibrium of consciousness and matter is reached in man. The emphasis thereafter is no longer on physical evolution but on the flowering of consciousness. According to *The Secret Doctrine* the shift toward more intense conscious life has already been attained and we have just begun the upward thrust. We have passed the most separative, differentiated phase of our long cycle and have just begun to move back toward conscious unity. This pivotal point in evolution is taking place deep in the consciousness of each of us.

Since man has dominated the scene on earth, physical evolution has nearly come to a halt except for minor variations. No major new species are known to have emerged during the last few million years. Many eminent thinkers agree that evolution has taken on an entirely different character and is now psychological and cultural rather than biological. As Alfred Korzybski, the father of General Semantics, pointed out, man has a unique mode of evolution. He is a "time binder"; that is, he passes on his achievements from one generation to the next by means of language. Human evolution is based on culture rather than genetics. This has allowed man to evolve at a phenomenal rate, far faster than the slow genetic changes that governed prehuman evolution.

Self-Consciousness

One uniquely human characteristic is our ability to observe ourselves, our thoughts and feelings, to mentally step outside the immediate situation and evaluate it. In other words, we are *self-conscious*. This capacity has led to other uniquely human abilities. It has enormously increased our power of choice, based on planning and anticipating the future. Choice leads to an altogether new degree of responsibility for our actions. Self-consciousness also underlies language and the use of symbols, mathematics, music, and abstract thought.

According to theosophy this dramatic leap, not yet fully actualized, was not inherited from man's predecessors in evolution. Rather it introduced a new dimension of evolution implanted in the human organism from a spiritual source. The physician-philosopher Le Comte du Nouy suspected this:

> . . . there seems to be an intellectually impassable gap be-tween the evolution of life and that of Man as such. Man is still an animal by his very structure . . . . Nevertheless he has also brought into the world from an unknown source, other instincts and ideas specifically human which have become overwhelmingly important . . .[20]

H.P.B. states that the awakening of mind in man resulted from a new fusion of the Divine Mind into nature. Though divine Intelligence is diffused throughout all nature, in man's mind there is a more direct focus, a new, more intimate con-nection with the physical world. Man is the carrier of Divine Mind in a way not found in other kingdoms. It functions more fully within his consciousness and inner being.

The full impact of this new dimension lies far in the future; the inner potential of our minds is still only very partially developed. The biologist Theodosius Dobzhansky believes that the development of our potentialities is "far from ex-hausted . . . . Man must develop as the bearer of spirit and of ultimate concern."

Future Unfoldment

Psychologists today agree that it is normal to continue to grow and unfold during adulthood. The humanistic psy-chologist Abraham Maslow studied this process, and Jung perceived individuation as the major direction for human growth. Teilhard de Chardin saw mankind as a whole moving toward further "hominization," becoming more human. These are lesser versions of the theosophical doctrine of the gradual realization and expression of man's innate powers. We glimpse the direction of human growth in such forerunners of the mainstream of mankind as Plato, Einstein, Leonardo, Jesus, Buddha. Geniuses in all fields throughout history not only leave us the heritage of their creative insights. They also reveal the possibilities of the human mind, possibilities all of us will one day unfold. In future eons thousands and tens of thousands, even millions of years hence, we will develop powers of mind, intuition, and will undreamed of in our present state.

We now stand at the turning point of evolution. Up to man's emergence, evolution was unconscious and automatic, propelled by the impetus of the Divine Mind on passive, receptive nature. With the birth of self-consciousness, we ourselves gained the power to become agents of evolution. Because we can choose our inner feelings and thoughts, we have the possibility of self-control and self-direction. This gives us some control over our environment and our world. Our evolution is now self-induced through our own decisions and efforts. Although the full development of self-consciousness and choice is not yet apparent, we are capable to some extent of choosing what we wish to express and be and what our world will be. We can begin consciously to direct our own evolution, both as a species and individually.

As we seldom think of the eonic development behind our present state of being, so, encapsulated in the present moment, we do not see the immense potential that lies ahead. Every capacity and ability destined to evolve in future mankind already lies latent within each of us now. Every potential of the One, of the Divine Mind, is present from the beginning, only awaiting the proper time and setting to emerge into manifestation. We have untold potentialities within.

We do not have to wait for nature's time table to unfold. We can even now begin to quicken our inner growth and development. We can stretch our minds to understand great principles and thus develop higher strata of thought. We can also reach into the intuitive realm through deep contemplation and silent meditation to find a source of unlearned wisdom within. We can try to universalize our attitudes towards others, experience each as an expression of the One Life at a particular level of unfoldment, and begin to actualize universal love and compassion. As we work consciously to develop our mental and spiritual capacities, we move in the direction of the whole cosmic evolutionary process.

This inner quickening, known as the Path (chapter 15), is dealt with in yoga and in all religions. Oliver Wendell Holmes perceived its action in the way the two poles of consciousness and form work within us as we grow inwardly. He compared our consciousness, expanding within its sheath, to a chambered nautilus, which grows larger and larger chambers to inhabit as it expands:

> Build thee more stately mansions, O my soul,
> As the swift seasons roll!
> Leave thy low-vaulted past!
> Let each new temple, nobler than the last,
> Shut thee from heaven with a dome more vast,
> Till thou at length are free,
> Leaving thine outgrown shell by life's unresting sea![21]

13

Karma

As no cause remains without its due effect from
greatest to least, from a cosmic disturbance down to
the movement of your hand, and as like produces
like, Karma is that unseen and unknown law which
adjusts wisely, intelligently, and equitably each effect
to its cause, tracing the latter back to its producer.

The Secret Doctrine

*K*arma, the concept of cause and effect from Buddhism
and Hinduism, has become widely known in the West,
as it has always been in the Orient. The word has found its
way into conversations among people at all levels of Western
society and has even shown up in popular music. However,
most people familiar with the idea think of it as shaping our
personal lives, as "paying us back" for our actions, good and
bad. This perhaps is the realm in which karma seems closest
to us. Yet karma is a universal law inherent in the One and
encompasses all of manifestation, all kingdoms of nature,
from atoms to galaxies, from rocks to human beings. H.P.B.
assures us that "every creature is subject to Karma"[1] and "no
spot in the manifested universe is exempt from its sway."[2]

She states that "the One Life is closely related to the One
Law which governs the world of Being—Karma,"[3] and that
this is "the *Ultimate Law* of the Universe." She says that it
"exists from and in eternity, truly, for it is eternity itself."[4] Its

reaches are far greater than our human affairs. Like all the principles outlined in esoteric philosophy, karma is an aspect of the one nonmaterial Reality that comes into play as manifestation proceeds. Karma as the law of cause and effect is involved in all differentiation and all relationships, spiritual as well as physical. Therefore, it must have become active at the awakening of the universe with the polarization of consciousness and matter. The first manifestation of cause and effect occurred when consciousness as Divine Mind began to create a world by impressing organization on precosmic matter. This, presumably, is the beginning of karmic action, which continues on every level of being throughout the entire cycle of manifestation.

> At the first flutter of renascent life . . . 'the Mutable Radiance of the Immutable Darkness unconscious in Eternity' passes, at every new birth of Kosmos, from an inactive state into one of intense activity . . . it differentiates, and then begins its work through that differentiation. This work is Karma.[5]

H.P.B. defines karma as "the unerring law which adjusts effect to cause on the physical, mental, and spiritual planes of being."[6] She depicts it as a law of harmony that continually restores the naturally harmonious state of the cosmos whenever it becomes disturbed. "The only decree of Karma —an eternal and immutable decree—is absolute harmony in the world of Matter as it is in the world of Spirit."[7] Karma "restores disturbed equilibrium in the physical and broken harmony in the moral world."[8] She compares it to a bough which "bent down too forcibly, rebounds with corresponding vigor."[9] Thus karma appears not as an external law acting from the outside but as an elastic quality of the cosmos itself, which causes it to spring back into harmony when distorted.

The Secret Doctrine does not depict karma mechanically or as "an eye for an eye" doctrine as some later writers have interpreted it. H.P.B. does not predict a one-to-one relationship between cause and effect—a predetermined course in which certain types of actions always have the same karmic consequences. In her view karma is not a mechanical system in which engaging a gear moves a cam, that in turn eventually turns a wheel, in a prescribed, linear, cause-and-effect manner. This kind of causality implies a rigid determinism—an unalterable sequence of events—which is not in keeping with theosophical philosophy. Rather, karma is fluid and flexible, as outcomes are continually shaped by the input of new factors. "Karma does not act in this or that particular way always."[10] Rather it works in an interconnected system in which everything affects everything else.

The workings of karma might be compared to the complexities of weather patterns. Huge areas of high and low pressure swirl through the atmosphere replacing one another, causing winds and many atmospheric conditions. Moisture from the earth rises and forms clouds, which may blow hundreds of miles before releasing their moisture as rain or snow. The jet stream high above the earth has an effect, as do deserts created centuries ago by nomadic peoples who overgrazed their herds. Seas of blacktop and concrete in modern cities play a part. The weather at a given place on a given day results from a combination of innumerable factors, past and present, local and distant, and new influences keep entering the system to change the outcome. Karma, too, is multidimensional, not linear. It is affected by and works on physical, mental, and spiritual levels, on all the planes and fields of nature. It brings into play influences from the distant past as well as those of the moment. Though determined by the past, the future is far from set. It is the result of countless causes. Prem and Ashish bring out the wholeness within which karma works:

> No *thing* causes any other thing, for causality resides not in things but in the whole. Particular events take place not because of any power in some other events which are said to be their causes, but because of an organic linking of the whole of cosmic experience, a linkage which is such that all events in the Cosmos are bound together in one harmonious correlation. Movement of any one "part" or element of the Cosmos necessitates movements of all the other elements, not because of any direct "causal power" exerted by the first but because all exist together in one seamless garment that is the Whole.[11]

Karma is involved in the vast sweeps of cyclic life that

wheel behind evolution, which are "pre-ordained, so to say, by Karmic law."[12] While the law of cycles sets manifestation going in recurrent patterns, it is karma that fashions the specific events within the cycles.

> [It is] the mysterious guiding intelligent power, which gives the impulse to and regulates the impetus of cycles and universal events . . . . Karma's visible adjuster on a grand scale.[13]

Karma connects each cycle of manifestation to all the previous ones, as "the working of Karma [is] in the periodical renovations of the universe."[14] The geological ages, the birth and death of species and kinds of plants and animal life, the coming and going of great races of men, the rise and fall of civilizations are all involved in karmic continuity. "There is a predestination in the geological life of our globe, as in the history, past and future, of races and nations. This is closely connected with what we call Karma."[15] It embodies what might be called a law of universal conservation—ensuring that nothing is lost, that the fruits of one cycle are passed on to the next.

Individual Karma

Karma also acts intimately and precisely in the affairs of individuals. While cosmic karma rolls on in grand cycles, individual karma gathers together tendencies and discharges them as events in our lives and evokes our inherent characteristics, whether physical, emotional, or intellectual. We all receive the repercussions of our own acts and thoughts, our personal karma. Just as each person has an individual scent which can be detected by a dog, it seems that each individual can be "sniffed out" by forces of karma. In the unimaginably complex karmic currents set up by humanity, in some mysterious way our own waves ripple out and return precisely to us. H.P.B. likens the process to the effects created by a stone falling into a pond and setting up waves which roll back and forth until equilibrium is restored, and the pond is again quiet. All action, no matter on what level, produces such disturbances.

> But since each disturbance starts from some particular point, it is clear that equilibrium and harmony can only be restored by the reconverging *to that same point* of all the forces which were set in motion from it. And here you have proof that the consequences of a man's deeds, thoughts, etc., must all react upon *himself* with the same force with which they were set in motion.[16]

According to esoteric philosophy, as humanity won through to the higher levels of mind and became capable of choice, individuals became responsible for their actions in a way not possible among lower animals. With this responsibility came personal karma. According to this doctrine, we ourselves are responsible for our lives, for our circumstances, our pain and joy, our opportunities and limitations, even our character traits, talents, neuroses and personality blockages. Everything about us is the outcome of forces we ourselves have set in motion, either in this life or in some distant past. We are "under the empire of [our] self-made destiny."[17] Karma has given us back the actual consequences of our own actions. The way we live, our actions and thoughts, enter a continuous stream of causes that determine our lives. Nothing is lost. All the thoughts, motives, emotions which we generated in the past have gone into the complex strains that make us what we are today. "It is not . . . karma that rewards or punishes us, but it is we who reward and punish ourselves."[18]

However, as karma works with cycles and evolution on the grand scale, so does it work with evolution to promote growth in our individual lives. It "adjusts wisely, intelligently, and equitably each effect to its cause,"[19] reflecting our past actions in our outer lives and in our inner make-up. Thus our lives give us feedback, if we know how to read it, showing us a record of how we are doing, what is going well, where we have erred and failed. Because of karma we can learn from life.

It must be stressed, however, that karma is not fatalism or determinism. Prem and Ashish point out that our lives are neither absolutely determined nor absolutely free. We live according to "a determined track within whose unformed potentiality lies the opportunity for change and growth."[20] We cannot erase influences we generated in the past, but we can influence the course of our lives at any time by pouring in new energies in new directions. We may not see the results immediately, but karma assures that they will come, as any energy we generate must have its effect. Scanning our lives for recurrent patterns can reveal the areas in which we need to work. If we repress harmful tendencies, try to eliminate defects, and counteract negative elements within us, we set up new causes which alter the karmic outcome of past actions. Any help we offer others, any service we perform for worthwhile causes, any helpful, positive thoughts and emotions we send out will affect the karmic balance. In this realm right motives, feelings, and thoughts are more important even than right action, for energies from higher planes or fields are more powerful than physical energies. According to H.P.B.:

> It is a law of occult dynamics that a given amount of energy expended on the spiritual or astral plane is productive of far greater results than the same amount expended on the physical objective plane of existence.[21]

Thus love and hate are powerful factors in fashioning our karma.

Karmic Interconnections

H.P.B.'s exposition of karma also includes group and national karma. The strands of our individual karma are interwoven with those of our nation and other groups with which we have strong ties. All social evils are karmic, as are social opportunities. We each participate karmically in the actions of our nation, whether we like those actions or not. As groups are interdependent in a society and nations are interdependent in the world, each individual is in some ways karmically linked with all others, and we all share in the outcome of world events.

Thus in a sense our actions do affect all mankind. We tend to see our lives as in a limited sphere, our influence extending only to those in our immediate vicinity. But, as we have seen, the universe is not created from isolated bits. It is a vast network of interconnections in all directions, at all levels. Our actions do not stop at the periphery of our vision but affect the whole of life in some measure, one way or another.

In *Light on the Path*, a mystical work by Mabel Collins, there is a small essay on karma attributed to a great sage and Master. He likens the individual life to a rope composed of innumerable fine threads. From time to time some of these threads get caught or attached to something, creating a tangle and disorder in the whole. Sometimes one or more of the threads becomes stained, and the stain spreads and discolors other strands. But in time the threads pass out of the shadow into the shine, where they become golden and lie together straight and even. At last harmony is established. This revealing image illustrates the holistic nature of karma. The essay goes on to say:

> What it is necessary first to understand is not that the future is arbitrarily formed by any separate acts of the present, but that the whole of the future is in unbroken continuity with the present, as is the present with the past.[22]

As each individual life is composed of intertwined threads, so the whole of humanity is composed of individual lives intertwined and continually influencing one another. To the degree that we deliberately try to improve the energies we contribute to the whole, so in this world of interconnections will we be able to "lift a little of the heavy karma of the world."

III

Human Nature and the Human Journey

14

The Self and Its Spheres

As [the cosmic planes of substance] are seven in ONE,
so are we seven in ONE—that same absolute Soul of
the World, which is both Matter and non-Matter,
Spirit and non-Spirit, Being and non-Being. Impress
yourselves with this idea, all those of you who would
study the mysteries of SELF.

H. P. Blavatsky

*H*ow little we know of ourselves! In our waking consciousness we peer through a narrow slit that screens
out the largest part of the world and of our own inner nature.
By far the greatest part of our being lies in the shadowy
depths of our unconscious. We use only a small portion of
our limitless capacities. As William James once said:

Our normal waking consciousness is but one special type of
consciousness, while all about it parted from it by the
filmiest of screens there lie potential forms of consciousness
entirely different. We may go through life without suspect-
ing their existence, but apply the requisite stimulus and at a
touch they are there in all their completeness.[1]

Theosophy takes into account many strata in man's consciousness. The theosophical image of man is on a grand
scale, far larger than the transient, too often petty concerns
which tend to eclipse our horizons. According to this view,
we are like the fabled African baobab tree which appears to

grow down from its uppermost parts and have its roots in heaven. We spring from the divine Ground which gives rise to all. Theosophy sees man as an infinite spiritual potential, the Self or Atman, as the Hindus call it, or the "spirit" of the Christians. This Self is never cut off from our transcendent roots in the pure Consciousness of the One.

Atman, the Deepest Self

Atman is pure consciousness uncolored by any experience or conditioning from any level. It is simple, clear awareness which cannot be divided or compartmentalized into "your consciousness" and "my consciousness." As H.P.B. says, "Consciousness (as such) is ubiquitous and can be neither localized nor centered in any particular subject, nor can it be limited."[2] Thus Atman appears as the universal, continuous, indivisible field, but somehow at the same time it is discrete, dimensionless points in that field. We might imagine an infinite field of radiance which becomes focused in numberless points of light, as stars seem to gather and focus the expanse of predawn light. As Atman, each of us is a point of consciousness in the field of divine Consciousness. Emily Sellon puts it thus:

> The universal consciousness or spirit which is the essence of all life constitutes the point of individual consciousness or ultimate being in every man, his fundamental identity with the One or the All—for consciousness is a "singular of which the plural is unknown."[3]

Atman is paradoxically ever united with the One and at the same time the essence of individual existence.

As the baobab tree sprouts down from heaven, so we grow earthward from our spiritual roots. We, as Atman turned toward the manifested world, take on a complex psychophysical organism through which to function. As explained in chapter 11, we are complex beings composed of several interpenetrating fields. Each of these has its unique characteristic which expresses an aspect of the divine potential. However, the many powers and capacities which flower in us are not confined to humanity but rather are our expression of universal principles that operate through all nature. That human nature expresses universal nature is obvious in our physical bodies, in which the laws of physics, chemistry, and biology are at work. It is less obvious at the superphysical levels, which cannot be known through our physical senses. However, seers and clairvoyants through the ages have confirmed the teaching of the Ancient Wisdom that the visible, physical aspect of man and nature is only the outer sphere of a series of living, vital, radiant realms which exist in and through the physical world. In contrast to the nonmaterial Reality which generates them, these spheres which exist in space and time have some degree of materiality, though more rarefied than the familiar physical world.

The Physical-Emotional-Mental Self

Closest to the physical is the vital or etheric level, in which man has a vehicle called the "etheric double." From this level streams of energy course through the physical body, energizing it and profoundly affecting our health. This energy, known in many cultures, has been called Ki, Ch'i, prana. Illness is associated with congestion or disrhythm in this vital stream. Acupuncture, therapeutic touch, and many other alternate forms of healing manipulate this energy. We can become sensitive to the energetic flow in our bodies. For example, we can experience the difference before and after healthful exercise, or feel how breathing techniques alter its streaming. Clairvoyants and seers who have developed their sensitivity to the superphysical worlds tell us that vital energy exists in abundance in nature. We can ingest it from trees as we open ourselves to their harmony, rootedness, and streaming energy. Natural bodies of water are also said to be charged with buoyant energy, which we absorb when we are near or in them. The vital level is the energetic side of physical nature and of ourselves, and we continuously exchange vitality with the environment at this level. H.P.B. uses the analogy of a sponge immersed in an ocean; the water is prana, the sponge is a living being. Prana, the breath of life as she calls it, "is the motor principle of life."[4]

The etheric body is interpenetrated by the emotional or

feeling aspect of our being, which is a manifestation of Atman in the psyche. This is what might be called the psychic element in nature, sensate, busy, craving. It expresses an aspect of the Real which is fluidic, incessantly flowing, ever-changing. Animals and even plants partake of this psychic element in some degree. This quality is embodied in the restless feelings that pulse through us in an endless stream of changing emotions. Here lie many of life's most prominent opposites, the drama of life, the intense human experiences of despair and elation, victory and defeat, love and hate. More of this emotional experience than we might at first suspect turns out to be based on sensation—liking, wanting, attraction to what is pleasant, avoiding, disliking, being repelled by the painful or unpleasant. Both emotions and sensations, when they are intense, intrude forcibly on our consciousness. They give variety and vivid contrasts to life. But even in our quiet moments there is some background of emotionality, however gentle, however unaware of it we may be.

The surges of emotion that we experience as anger, affection, depression, and excitement are actual waves of energy, finer than the etheric. Our feelings produce patterns of colors and rhythms that have been observed by clairvoyants in our emotional or astral field, often called the aura. This aura consists in part of astral and emotional matter that extends beyond the body about eighteen inches in an ovoid or egg shape. As our feelings change, the colors and rhythms in the aura change. Feelings we repeat over and over produce semipermanent patterns in this field. We also project our emotional energies into the larger field around us, where they can bombard other people, setting up similar rhythms in them. Conversely, more often than we know our moods are the result of influences from the larger field around us. We all influence one another at this emotional level, and we are vulnerable to nationwide and worldwide emotional influences such as anxiety and fear at times of crisis. Our best defense is, through practice, to learn to radiate positive feelings like love, good will, and joy. Doing so not only protects us from disturbances in the surrounding field, but also contributes to helping others through the field.

The mind is another field or vehicle in which Atman operates and by which it contacts the world. The universal mental field is expressed not only in humans but, like the other fields, throughout nature. It reflects the aspect of the Real which is characterized by order and organization, the Divine Mind.

The more mundane levels of mental energies (manas) interpenetrate and interact with emotional energies, so that thoughts, feelings, and bodily reactions work together. This aspect of the mind is restless and changeable, as our thoughts move along with the rise and fall of emotions and our attractions and aversions. H.P.B., following the tradition of Indian philosophy, called this *desire-mind* or *kama-manas.* It is symbolized in Indian literature as the monkey, curious, flitting from this to that, really part of the psyche. This concrete mind, as it has been called, also has a practical bent in solving everyday problems, using logic, at least to some extent. Through it we make schedules and order and organize our lives. At this level also lies the faculty that sorts and judges our sense impressions and interprets what we experience through our senses. As social psychologist Wilbur Schramm points out, "We *structure* experience so as to make it meaningful to us."[5] The structuring involves analysis and discrimination, stressing differences and separateness.

According to esoteric philosophy, thought, too, is energy and it creates "thought forms" or semipermanent structures in the subtle, superphysical "stuff" of the mental field or plane. These forms often remain as patterns within our mental field, where they color and influence much of our thinking. We also may emit them so that they affect others.

Ego in the sense of a separated self originates at this level of concrete mind. This is the ordinary little self of which we are normally conscious. Ken Wilber, a writer on Eastern and Western psychology, defines ego as "that band of consciousness that comprises our role, our picture of ourself, our self-image, as well as the analytical and discriminatory nature of the intellect."[6] Ego is our inner concept of ourselves which arises from the faculty of the concrete mind to divide, separate, categorize, see differences. This faculty places the notion of ourselves into a special category apart and separate from all else. Thus it solidifies and concretizes at a lower level the primordial split between subject and object, consciousness and matter. In Wilber's words, ego is the "fruition of the separate-self sense born with the primary dualism."[7]

Our ego rests largely on past experience and memory, as we gradually build a concept of what we are through our experience and relationships. It is "a bag of edited memories," as Wilber describes it. We unconsciously identify with this self-image and shut ourselves off from our larger capacities and vision and other elements of the Self. The ego also encloses us in an illusory cocoon where we feel distinct from and cut off from all else as we "mistake this relative point of reference for the real and permanent center of ourselves," as Lama Govinda put it.[8] It is possible to transcend the ego and live without its limitations, and thus attain far greater freedom and self-expression. We will explore such transcendence in chapter 15 on Self-Transformation.

Mind, the Pivot

The mind, however, has a double role. In addition to its concrete aspect, the seat of the ego, which is largely concerned with our personal lives and affairs, it has a universal aspect (Manas) which is "undisturbed by egoism, unruffled by distinctions, desires and aversions,"[9] according to Lama Govinda. In contrast to kama-manas, desire-mind, this level is *Buddhi-manas*. Its function has to do with abstract, conceptual thought, with synthesizing, with discovering unifying principles, rather than dissecting and separating, as does the concrete mind. It is the source of inspiration and creative insight, whether scientific, mathematical, philosophical, or artistic. Illumined by the intuition, this universal aspect of mind reveals life's deeper meanings. It can give us a sense of exhilaration as we contemplate principles and laws which govern the universe. This is the realm of universal truth—of Plato's Good, True, and Beautiful. Few people have developed the full potential of this aspect of the Self, but throughout history we see outstanding examples of its potential in the geniuses in every field who have contributed to the advance of culture.

The unique human capacity for self-consciousness has its roots at this level of the mind. Only we humans can step outside our own mind, as it were, and watch it in action. As Rollo May, the Existential psychologist, claimed, "the capacity to transcend the immediate situation is the basic and unique characteristic of human existence."[10] All we need do is focus our attention on our inner processes, the stream of thoughts, feelings, sensations. In the act of observing the operation of our mind, we as subject objectify even our own thoughts and feelings. The subject-object split draws a line between our consciousness and our inner mental processes. Thus we can actually glimpse that we are consciousness embedded in vehicles or fields, the Self in the emotional and mental bodies. However, we tend to identify with the vehicles and their highly individual set of interwoven habit patterns. We feel we *are* our attitudes, preferences, habitual emotions, etc. Self-consciousness gives rise to ego, and we cut ourselves off from Atman, which is never separate from the One, and enclose ourselves within its limited expression in the world. We forget our heavenly roots and confine our attention to side branches.

It is this ability of the mind to observe itself that makes possible abstract thought and the use of symbols. As we can detach ourselves from the flow of experiences, we can attach symbols to them. Whole realms of peculiarly human activity such as language, mathematics, and music are based on the ability to symbolize. Dealing with symbols is a typically human function. Even the word *man* is derived from the Sanskrit word *manas*, mind, implying our unique nature as thinker and symbol-maker.

Rollo May also stresses the capacity to transcend the immediate situation—"to stand outside and look at one's self and the situation [gives the power] to assess and guide one's self by an infinite variety of possibilities."[11] This is the source of our ability to foresee the outcome of our actions and plan for the future by manipulating symbols mentally. It gives us the power of choice and therefore makes us responsible for our actions.

H.P.B. places our ability for self-consciousness in an evolutionary setting. Atman or spirit on its own plane is not self-conscious, nor are creatures less evolved than humans. Mind or Manas is necessary to focus Atman, a ray of the one divine light.

> There is no potentiality for creation or Self-Consciousness, in a pure Spirit on this our plane unless its too homogeneous, perfect—because divine—nature is mixed with and strengthened by an essence already differentiated. It is [Manas] that can furnish this needed consciousness on the plane of differentiated Nature.[12]

Thus, Manas is the seat of our individuality as well as the gateway to unity. Looking down, it solidifies the separated self and ego; looking up it unites us with the All.

Intuitive Insight

As the mental field permeates and interpenetrates the emotional field in the aura, so the field of intuition, Buddhi, permeates them both. The word *intuition* does not convey the full meaning of this Sanskrit term. *Buddhi* connotes the principle within us which is closest to Atman and therefore characterized by unity. It includes expansive, unitary feeling experience and also a kind of insight through fusion. It contrasts with the concrete mind which pigeonholes, separates, and labels. This latter has been called the "concretizing" mind because of its tendency to pin things down and make them more concrete. By contrast, Buddhi imparts a living, dynamic, fresh way of knowing that is charged with a kind of joy. It yields knowledge which is direct and immediate, intimate, often sudden, not abstract and verbal or inferential. William James is one among many philosophers who have recognized two ways of knowing things, "knowing them immediately or intuitively, or knowing them conceptually or representatively."[13]

Brain researchers have found these two types of knowing correspond in a general way to the left and right hemispheres of the brain. The left hemisphere corresponds to manasic or mental functions: words, symbols, concepts, ideas. It is analytical, discrete, and rational. The right hemisphere is more wholistic, as it grasps the gestalt and synthesizes. It is intuitive: it processes direct, immediate perceptions not mediated by symbols, such as spatial sense or painting or the rhythms of music and dance. In the theosophical view, these experiences are not necessarily the direct experience of Buddhi itself at its own level but rather the reflection of its quality at lower levels.

In direct knowledge by intuition, we merge or fuse with the object of the knowledge and come to understand it from within rather than thinking about it from outside. We all experience such merging in peak moments of losing ourselves in something beautiful, in deep empathy with someone so that for the moment we see from his or her view point, or in so fully understanding an idea that we feel united with it. V. K. Chari, a student of Eastern philosophy and religion, describes intuition from the point of view of Vedanta: "Intuitive experience is a form of mergence, a dissolution of the 'other' sense in pure consciousness." He goes on to explain further:

> Intuition is knowledge by identity. In that state of immediacy the object is merged with the subject, so that the subject is all. The knower, known, and the act of knowing are one. Thus, in intuition all dualities are dissolved.[14]

In the experience of Buddhi we drop our notion of ourselves as cut off from all else and merge consciousness with its object in an experience of unity. Mystic union with the All is the highest form of Buddhic experience, but Buddhi is also expressed in ways that are more mundane and in creative insight at every level. Philosopher-scientist Michael Polyani speaks of it as an intimation of truth or "tacit knowledge" that steers a scientist into a fruitful line of research. Einstein acknowledges its importance in the process of discovery:

> The intellect has little to do on the road to discovery. There comes a leap in consciousness, call it intuition or what you

will, and the solution comes to you and you don't know
how or why.[15]

Brian Josephson, a physicist and Nobel laureate who has
turned his research to consciousness and psycholinguistics,
states that in scientific work, "It's much more a matter of get-
ting the intuition of how things are and then thinking through
to see whether the intuition fits the facts."[16]

Josephson's statement points up the relation between intuition and intellect. The Buddhic insight must be verified by the
mind, meshed with other sources of knowledge, and articulated in understandable terms. To be of value, it must be
anchored in the structure of the mind. I.K. Taimni sees the
unification of intuition and mind when he speaks of Buddhi
or intuition as "the illuminating power behind the mind."

In addition to unifying the thinker with the object of
thought, intuitive insight working with the abstract mind generates a kind of knowledge that is unitive: it synthesizes and
sees relationships within a whole. Intuition operates in science, art, philosophy, and one's relationships with others. It
takes us out of the center of our world and gives an overall perspective, with our ego in its rightful place in a larger whole.
Chari expresses clearly the unitive function of intuition:

> Intuition is integral knowledge. The vision it gives is the
> vision of the whole, a unified, synoptic vision of reality, in
> which the inner and outer, the one and the many, the in-
> dividual and the universal, are perceived as one.[17]

Intuition differs from the psychic hunch in that it originates
in a more spiritual aspect of the Self and is not concerned with
our smaller selfish interests. True intuitive insight is direct
cognition through unification, while in psychic flashes the
subject is still separate from the object. Though psychic
knowledge can be valid and useful in its own sphere, it cannot
convey the numinous, unitive quality of Buddhi.

The deeper levels of our being—Buddhi and Manas—also
radiate energies into the surrounding field as we use them.
Though these subtler energies are quiet, never tempestuous,
they are more powerful than those of the emotions and concrete mind. Emitting energies at these levels can be far more

helpful to ourselves and others than can positive emotional and mental energies alone.

The Spiritual Will

The term *Atma* is used to express the Atman, the essential Self, as it turns outward toward the manifested world, so to speak. Although Atman is the substratum of all that exists, including all the levels and planes within us, *Atma* can be considered a principle of man and a level of human consciousness. We experience it as the very sense of self, the core of our being, the pure center of awareness stripped of all conditioning, all coloring. Taimni refers to it as "the transcendent principle within us which forms, as it were, the very heart and core of our being."[18]

In addition, Atma has been referred to as the spiritual will. It is our individual localization of the life of the One, our point in the limitless universal field. As such, Atma is a focus of divine power, the creative energy that generates all manifestation. Taimni describes it by a metaphor of electricity:

> [Atma] is the plug point, as it were, connecting the set of vehicles belonging to a particular soul with the Power House, through which the power needed by the soul for different purposes can be taken.[19]

The spiritual will is characterized by power and strength which sweep away obstacles. A person in whom it is active is self-determined and directs his or her life from within, not swayed by whims and lesser aims. Such a person lives by guiding ideals and transmits them into physical expression. Albert Schweitzer is an example. He gave up a brilliant career in music and became a physician so that he could serve those less fortunate in Africa. His life was one-pointed, wholly devoted to the ideal of *ahimsa*, harmlessness.

Desire can be thought of as a reflection of the spiritual will at the emotional level, and it shows some of the qualities of the spiritual will. However, desire is often selfish and self-centered rather than seeking the overall good, as does the spiritual will. Atma is the driving force behind all our vehicles, though we seldom if ever experience its power on its own level in pure form. Still, it is not distant and unreachable but rather the very foundation of our being at every level.

The Whole Self

Each of our vehicles has a life of its own, its special quality. Each beyond the physical is composed of a unique grade of superphysical matter. Yet all these fields are bound together and operate as a whole. Yoga philosophy describes chakras or "wheels" of energy, through which influences pass from one level or field to another. There are seven of these centers located within the body, from the base of the spine to the top of the head. Clairvoyants report that each is characterized by a dynamic geometry and significant colors that rotate through the chakra. They influence the glands and nervous system, which also influence them, and they bind together the physical, etheric, and emotional levels. Chakras also channel energies between the highest levels and the physical. Meditation and yoga activate these centers so that interchange between the spiritual and the physical is stepped up.

We are indeed complex beings embodying many kinds of universal energy, truly microcosms. There are subtle ranges in our nature which we have at best only glimpsed. Contrasts, opposites, and rich variety lie within us. Yet at the same time each of us is a whole person, not a loosely knit set of vehicles. We integrate many strains within ourselves, and we as Atman, the Self, express through each of them. As we identify more and more with the inner Self and loosen the hold of the ego, we begin to take control of our various vehicles and direct them toward our true spiritual aims. As we contact less familiar layers of being within, we expand our range of expression and live ever more fully. Thus we begin to awaken the sleeping giant that lies within and call into activity the immense powers of our inner nature.

15

Self-Transformation

The heart is the dwelling place of that which is the
Essence of the universe . . . . If you draw aside the
veils of the stars and the spheres, you will see that all
is one with the Essence of your own pure soul.

Farid al-Din Attar

*A*ll life is moving, changing, developing, including our
own inner being. In this dynamic world ruled by the
universal principle of motion where nothing ever stays the
same, we too must keep flexible and flow with life's currents.
Life will not let us stand still. However, inner change need not
be haphazard and random; it can be real growth in which we
move to higher levels of integration and maturity. As with
Prigogine's dissipative structures, when we experience disorganization of old patterns within, we can move to a higher
level, a new and superior order. Inner change should conform
to what Chinese philosophy calls the law of change, which
regulates movements in a dynamic but orderly way. As the
orientalist Hellmut Wilhelm said, "The concept of change is
not an external, normative principle that imprints itself upon
phenomena; it is an inner tendency according to which development takes place naturally and spontaneously."[1] Just as
new orders emerge as the seed becomes the tree, so our inner

life reshapes itself naturally as we mature. We sometimes become acutely aware of the need for growth and change when we face a crisis after which we cannot remain as we were. But an inner pressure toward evolutionary growth in a constantly evolving universe is always present to some extent, though often submerged by the busyness of our lives.

It has long been recognized that we continue to grow psychologically after we reach adulthood. For centuries East Indians have supported *sannyasis*, men who have already earned a living and raised a family and in their later years are freed from worldly concerns to search for spiritual truth. In the West psychologists such as C. G. Jung and Abraham Maslow have demonstrated growth toward fulfilling inner potential in adults of all ages, and the psychiatrist Roberto Assagioli has made spiritual dimensions of growth more explicit. The stages of adult progression and their rites of passage—marriage, parenthood, mid-life crisis, etc.—have been plotted and discussed. Lawrence Kohlberg, following Jean Piaget's work on cognitive development, has described stages in moral development from early childhood through postadult maturity, and more recently James Fowler, a pastor and an educator at Emory University, has done the same for the development of mature faith. Humanistic and transpersonal psychology offers guidelines and techniques for psychological and spiritual unfoldment of adults. All of these approaches recognize that a person who is not growing and developing is generally unhappy and dissatisfied, for continuous growth is necessary to our fulfillment as humans.

These dynamic growth psychologies are in keeping with theosophical philosophy, which places humanity in a context of continuing evolution. As we have seen, mankind is unfinished, and both the individual and the human species as a whole are unfolding new powers, new ways of perceiving, new mental and spiritual potentials. Change occurs sometimes in sudden spurts when we can almost see new growth spring up like mushrooms after a summer rain, or sometimes it may happen in imperceptible increments in the midst of seeming stagnation. Like the learning curve plotted when a new skill is being mastered, there are steps up, falling back, leveling off, new steps forward, but the general direction is always upward. As *Light on the Path* says, "The soul of man is immortal and its future is the future of a thing whose growth and splendor has no limit."[2]

As discussed in the previous chapter, we each have enormous untapped potentials. All the planes and principles of nature are already implanted in us. All that is needed for the fulfillment of evolution's long-range goals exists within us already, buried at some unconscious level of our being. In this darkness lies a realm of experience utterly different from our usual bright-daylight waking consciousness. We get intimations of this vast unexplored area, sometimes in significant dreams, sometimes in moments of clarity in meditation, or even in the rush of a hectic day when suddenly our mind, emotions, intuition, and will come into sharp focus in the face of a crisis. We hear "faint echoes from these inner regions [that] can evoke a feeble response in our mind and enable us to catch glimpses, here and there, of our transcendental nature," as Taimni put it.[3] We are like the starling, a drab and uninteresting little bird until the light hits just so and brilliant iridescent colors shine out.

Our Threefold Nature

We glimpsed the richness and complexity of our nature in the discussion of the levels and fields in us. All these various human qualities and functions, recognized in esoteric philosophy since antiquity, have been grouped and broken down differently in different systems of thought. Vedanta speaks of five *koshas* or sheaths, Raja Yoga recognizes four, Christians have the threefold division of spirit, soul, and body, whereas esoteric philosophy generally posits seven. Even in modern-day theosophical literature different arrangements can be found. They all agree, however, on three major divisions in human make-up—what can be called the personality, the soul, and the Self or Atma. In more recent theosophical literature the most familiar levels—physical, etheric, emotional, lower mental—are considered to coalesce in the *personality*, the familiar everyday self which we ordinarily perceive ourselves to be. This has been called the "lower self," but it is just as important and essential as any spiritual element. The more enduring aspect of the self has been called the soul, the higher self, or just the Self, the Reincarnating Ego or simply Ego (as opposed to ego, the root of egocentricity). This consists of the abstract mind, the intuition, and Atma, also referred to as Atma-Buddhi-Manas.

According to the esoteric teaching the higher self or soul endures from life to life and its potential is evoked over long periods by the experiences of the personalities it generates. H.P.B. says of this "spiritual soul," as she sometimes calls it, that it is "not a fleeting life. It is the man that was, that is, that will be."[4] Thus esoteric philosophy sees our true home as the level of the soul, from which we periodically project the more earthly aspects of ourselves into the lower worlds. We undergo life's infinitely varied experiences through many incarnations—sometimes a man, sometimes a woman, sometimes rich, sometimes poor, sometimes cultured, sometimes unskilled, sometimes in charge of others, sometimes powerless. Those with whom we have close ties keep reappearing in various relationships as karma continually draws us into environments and relationships determined by our past actions in which old energies can be played out, even as new ones are emitted. Sooner or later in each life, we are inevitably thrown into those situations and with those people that can open our capacities and challenge us to growth and change. The soul has been compared to a many-faceted jewel, with various incarnations revealing different of its facets.

Clairvoyants tell us that as we grow through many lifetimes, the vehicle of the soul at the abstract mental level (sometimes called the Causal Body) increases in size and brilliance. Here is the repository of the essence of all our experiences on earth after they have been assimilated and transformed into faculty and ability. From this point of view, what we recognize as talent is not accidental or God-given but a reflection of this level of the soul where faculty has been developed through long practice.

Our capacity for impersonal, universal thought and feeling is rooted at this level, as already discussed. Here also dwells what we might think of as our individual archetype or the divine Idea of ourselves, the unique flavor of what we are, the source of our inherent individuality, our special configuration of abilities and powers which will unfold and become actualized through time. In high moments the personality can open up to admit powers and influences from this level and for a time the archetype becomes integrated with the conscious self. We sometimes touch this inner power when we are using our capacities in a self-forgetful way, lost in work or deep thought or creativity. Occasionally we feel the touch of the soul at moments when we have a clear sense of direction which emanates from a sense of what we truly are. Virginia Burden, a lifelong student of the intuition, recognizes such experience:

> At times when you are very quiet and desire and emotion have become stilled, you can observe the quiet shaping of yourself from within. You can see the form you are intended to take, the work you should do—your function in the environment and the scheme of things . . . .[This] is a deep and intelligent observation of your own nature and propensities.[5]

Even deeper within than the level of the soul is our inmost essence, the Atma or eternal Self, the truly universal aspect of ourselves, our point in the divine Ground, never separated from the One. When combined with Buddhi as a sheath or nebulous contact with the world of manifestation, this is called in theosophical literature the *monad*, a term which sometimes also includes higher Manas. This way of classifying these higher principles overlaps somewhat with the concept of the soul. But Atma or the Self remains that which is truly eternal, our individual locus in the Divine that generates and expresses through the soul as the soul does through the personality.

Sometimes the intense focus of Atma breaks through to our conscious mind when we center ourselves, perhaps in meditation, when we feel all the energies and levels within us for the moment in balance and equilibrium around a deep, quiet center in the heart. Paradoxically, at such moments of focus we also feel an expansion, a unity—a momentary reflection in us of the oneness of the Self with the All. P. W. Martin, a Jungian psychologist, describes such an experience:

> [When one] discovers the deep center, makes the creative contact with the "More," undergoes the inward transforming experience, he has borne in upon him that consciousness is but part of a greater being—the whole spirit, the Self—the bulk of which exists in another realm.[6]

Thus, though we ordinarily experience ourselves as the personality, the most peripheral aspect of the Self, we also have flashes and intuitions of the soul and even of Atma, our inmost essence.

Between Two Worlds

At some point in our long journey through evolution, there comes a time for each of us when ordinary life becomes arid and inconsequential, when we yearn for something more, something richer, some new dimension of life. Then, perhaps after long dissatisfaction and suffering, we begin to take more seriously our intimations from the deeper layers of the Self. We discover, at first from others or through reading, that we can deliberately encourage our own growth, hasten evolution within our own consciousness, renew ourselves from deeper levels. Then as we resolve to begin a new life of training and realization, we enter what has been called the path, the way, Tao, dharma, individuation, self-actualization. It is a way that leads us beyond our commonplace self with its familiar joys and sorrows, frustrations and rewards, to new perceptions of what we are, fresh insight into our potential and what we can become. We may feel that we have been like night travelers in a storm with no vision of the road ahead until suddenly a lightning flash lights up our surroundings, and for a moment we clearly see our way. The vision starts us on the spiritual path, and we begin deliberately to train ourselves to release our hidden powers, to render our personality transparent to the light within.

The work of self-transformation on the path is to enlarge the scope of our consciousness to include all the levels of our being and to integrate all the layers and levels into a dynamic whole. The aim of evolution, which the path hastens, is to release all our potentials and place them at the service of the Self, which can then integrate the newly developed powers into its sphere of ever-expanding activity. Our unfoldment is not merely the awakening of spirituality but gaining the conscious use of all that is in us at every level.

The key to unlocking these deeper potentials lies in the dual nature of the mind. As already discussed, the abstract mind, Manas, is an aspect of the enduring part of ourselves, the soul, and is in tune with great ideas, abstract, universal concepts, which can grip us and carry us beyond the personal self. In a lower key, the concrete mind or manas is at the foundation of the personal, separate self. It sorts and judges our sense impressions and is dominated by desire and repulsion, likes and dislikes, our unique personal preferences and attitudes. This aspect of manas gives rise to the ego, as we have seen, to the notion of being an enclosed self separate from all others and all else. We mistake the relative point of reference in manas for the real and permanent center of ourselves.

The personal ego represents a necessary phase in the development of the individual, as of the species. In the cycle of involution, when man is becoming more deeply involved in materiality, the sharpness and even the narrowness of the concrete mind is needed to focus the diffuse energies of the higher levels, to anchor us in the physical world. Indeed, H.P.B. writes that very early prehistoric races of men were diffuse and inchoate, that it took eons to learn to function in and master the physical world. Thus the development of the concrete mind and the ego has its place in the scheme of evolution. Lama Govinda states that "Manas is the principle through which universal consciousness . . . descends into multiplicity."[7] The ego is a necessary phase in our evolution from inchoate, homogeneous spirit to a being with potentialities at all levels.

However, once we become "grounded," as it were, it is necessary that we break through the ego and egotism in order to release our inner potentials and expand the limits of our conscious life. As Carlo Suares says, the ego "must develop until it is strong enough to break its own shell through an inner, natural process of development." Thus we move from ineffective diffuse spirituality through focused, efficient materiality, to mastery and ability to focus in all realms. The whole of human evolution has been expressed as moving from unconscious perfection to conscious imperfection to conscious perfection, or as T. S. Eliot so beautifully put it:

> We shall not cease from exploration
> And the end of all our exploring
> Will be to arrive where we started
> And know the place for the first time.[8]

Thus mind is the principle that binds us to the world of the senses and the ego and also the principle that can liberate us. H.P.B. shows that Manas is the middle principle, the median between the highest and lowest, the spiritual and the physical. She speaks of the conscious mind as "the connecting link between Spirit and Matter, Heaven and Earth."[9] Lama Govinda echoes this when he says, "Manas is that element of our consciousness which holds the balance between the empirical-individual qualities on the one side and the universal-spiritual qualities on the other."[10] He gives an example of these two aspects of our mentality:

> The difference in the effect of these two directions may be compared to the vision of a man who observes the manifold forms and colours of a landscape and feels himself different from it (as 'I' and 'here')—and the vision of another one who gazes into the depth of the firmament, which frees him of all object-perception and thus from the awareness of his own self as well, because he is only conscious of the infinity of space or of 'emptiness'. His 'I' here loses its position through lack of contrast or opposition, finding neither anything to grasp nor from which to differentiate itself.[11]

Our work on the path is to harmonize these two aspects of mind and Self, to deliberately learn to open the personality so that it can resonate to the universal strains within. We need to erase the artificial line that separates us from the inner universal Self.

Letting Go

One of the key factors in this process is in cultivating impersonality and nonattachment. Such letting go does not mean being uncaring and impassive, without warmth or enthusiasm. It means rather not becoming overly identified with anything—our body, our convictions and opinions, our reactions, our feelings, even our loved ones, and most especially our self-image, that semiconscious picture we hold of what we are. In short, it means letting go of our tight hold on the ego. We can learn to have a light touch, not to cling too tenaciously to anything transient, not even ourselves. Psychologist Thomas Keefe describes the flexibility that comes with nonattachment:

> Nonattachment is not detachment or withdrawal. It is "cognitive flexibility" . . . an easy harmonizing of the self with changing realities and moment-to-moment events . . . . Most people experience it when they are functioning with full attention their full self—absorbed in the activity.[12]

Nonattachment opens us up to our cosmic connections, our interactions with our surroundings at all levels, and to our true identity with the One. It comes when we recognize that we and the world are constantly changing, that there are no abiding realities on the peripheral, outer levels of life, only in the unchanging universal principles and at the deep center which coincides with the timeless Reality of the One. When we truly realize this, we can begin to let go of the transient and look for permanence only at a deeper level of being.

H.P.B. stresses the importance of impersonality in *The Voice of the Silence:* "Thou hast to merge the two into the One and sacrifice the personal to Self impersonal and thus destroy the path between the two."[13] For the Self, the soul, cannot be confined to the small sphere of our self-interest but ranges wide into universals. We cannot expect to reach its grandeur and scope if we stay within the personal ego and its narrow concerns. H.P.B. tells us to "seek in the impersonal for the eternal man. Having sought him out, look within. Thou art Buddh."[14]

From Ego to Self

Numberless methods and disciplines have been developed and handed down through the ages to bring about this conquest of the Self. Every religion has a path or way for sincere aspirants who want to plunge deeper than do more superficial proponents. Prayer or meditation, self-evaluation, service, and study all have their place. All methods aim at two essential elements in self-transformation: purifying the personal self and shifting focus to a higher level.

Most of us are at least partially aware of our shortcomings —resentment, anger, anxiety, lack of persistence, lack of confidence, pride and conceit, jealousy, greed, narrowness of mind, etc. The Buddha subsumed all these under the categories of lust, greed, and anger and showed how they all stem from a false sense of ego, egotism, and overconcern with ourselves. Whether we choose the Middle Way of Buddhism, the "narrow way and strait gate" of Christianity, or any other way, our task is the same—somehow to uproot egotism, even its tenacious little hair roots that coil in our unconscious depths. We might have sudden breakthroughs, like the Zen meditator who laughs out loud as he pierces the riddle of his koan or the Christian who sheds tears of joy and relief when her cares first dissolve in the love of Christ. At other times growth may be painfully slow as we doggedly persist in coaxing the ego off center stage.

While we strive for the insight and practice the discipline required for this monumental task, we also try to elevate our focus of consciousness. Reading and contemplating great ideas, losing ourselves in beauty—music, art, nature—devoting ourselves to great causes, genuine compassion and concern for others—all these can take us out of ourselves and stretch us. Meditation, particularly if it leads to centering, can assist us in what the Buddha called "turning about in the deepest seat of consciousness," in which we turn from the outer world of the many to the inner world of the One. Any expansion or deepening we achieve will help put the ego in its rightful place of submission to the Self, while any vacuum left by displaced egotism will be filled from above by the Self.

This is a long and arduous process which will take more than one lifetime to complete, and it demands determination and perseverance, for as *The Mahatma Letters* says regarding the mastering of the self, "there is no such other difficult struggle."[15] But we are bound to succeed eventually for we are working with the thrust of the whole cosmos behind us. We are trying to bring about what evolution will accomplish only very slowly; we are harmonizing ourselves with the long-range purposes of all manifestation.

The influence of an Enlightened One such as the Buddha is "far-reaching, grown great and beyond measure."

There are those throughout history who have achieved, thus showing that our goals can be realized. Seers, initiates, wise ones through the ages have demonstrated the heights that the human potential can reach. Looking at the lives of the Christ, the Buddha, Plato, or Lao-tzu, we can glimpse the possibilities of human development. In addition, esoteric philosophy teaches that there have always been advanced spiritual beings, Masters, adepts, who work silently behind the scenes for the upliftment of humanity. These are super-human intelligences who long ago rose above ego and established themselves at the level of the soul from which they radiate great power to aid and stimulate humanity. Such were the teachers of H.P.B., the authors of *The Mahatma Letters*. They show us a glimpse of the snowy peaks that lie ahead as day by day our inner conquest takes us farther up the mountainside.

16

Man the Microcosm

The Universe is a man on a large scale.
Lao Tzu

One of the outstanding features of life in this technological age is alienation from nature, a feeling of being cut off, isolated. If we are city dwellers, we seldom have the chance to melt into the glow of a sunset, or lose ourselves in the infinity of a night sky, or focus on the perfect geometry of a wild flower. Most of our time is spent enclosed in buildings or conveyances from which we can only peer at nature "out there" through windows.

Yet we are an intrinsic part of nature, as much its child as a tree or a waterfall. Our bodies are of the very stuff of nature, and according to theosophy the self-consciousness in us is a flowering of consciousness which pervades all nature. Even our most uniquely human powers are expressions of universals. For the Ancient Wisdom depicts man as a microcosm, a miniature of the cosmos, embodying all its principles, energies, functions. According to The Secret Doctrine, "Man [is] the microcosm and miniature copy of the macrocosm."[1] At every level, from highest spirit to densest matter, we are

181

immersed in the universal process, at one with it, exchanging with it in numerous ways. Inherent in each of us are all the principles of nature.

We have seen how unity runs through our entire being. We are composed of wholes within wholes, from atoms to organ systems. Each of us is a whole, all the complex strains of our nature converging into a unitary being. We also share a unity with humankind and exchange with others in numberless ways, as we do with the environment. At a deeper level we are each rooted in the primordial Ground of the universe. Our most essential Self, the core of our being, is Atman, our particular germ of divinity that inheres in the One, the Source of all.

We have also seen that the basic polarity of consciousness and matter is prominent within us. Subjectively we feel ourselves to be apart from the objective world and even from the stream of sensations, thoughts, and feelings that arise within us. The subject-object, consciousness-matter split is at the very foundation of all our experience, for in man the two primordial poles of being are in balance. We embody both spirit and matter in our complex nature, sometimes in tension and conflict, sometimes in dynamic harmony. Man has been defined in esoteric philosophy as "that being in the universe . . . in whom highest Spirit and lowest Matter are joined together by intelligence."[2]

The *intelligence* that unites spirit and matter in us is the mark of man. As nowhere else in physical nature, the Divine Mind expresses itself through our own mental faculties. We express the ordering principle of the cosmos at every level, as we embody all grades of universal being, the seven distinctive fields or planes of nature. There is an "indissoluble union between Man and the Universe, rendered in seven different ways,"[3] as H.P.B. put it. But it is our mind, our inner principle of organization, abstracting, planning, conveying meaning, that is our most direct connection with Divine Mind. Any organization and order in our lives, in our society, in our art and science, in any human endeavor, reflects this universal principle of order. The capacity for thought is the distinguishing feature of our species.

The principle of cycles also is alive in us in many ways,

from our breathing and physiological processes to our reincarnations into the physical world, as we periodically take on
a physical body and psyche and then shed them for awhile in
a cycle of rest and ingestion between lives. It is karma along
with the higher, more spiritual aspects of our being, that
assures continuity from life to life. The pressure from our
higher nature evokes growth and moves us in the direction of
evolution, while the law of karma acts as life's teacher,
presenting us with the consequences of our past actions and
decisions. We are the present focus of evolution; the arrow
pointing toward the future can fly only from within our
minds and hearts.

Thus, all the principles that govern the universe and its
workings are forcefully present in us. We have cosmic connections. We embody universals. Though unique in many
ways, we are not apart from nature. Rather, it works in and
through us. We are the revelation of its possibilities. As
philosophy professor Jacob Needleman put it, "The laws that
govern this great range of energy within the self are the laws
that govern everything in the universe."[4]

This is why contemplating the principles behind the
universe can be a very intimate process involving the whole
person, not just the mind. Theosophical principles come alive
in the conscious mind, not by analyzing and pulling them
apart, but by reaching intuitively into them, thinking around
them, sinking into them, and waiting for their significance to
emerge as direct realization. This kind of deep study con-
forms to Plato's concept of education as remembering. As we
consider the universals in nature, we might invoke the faint,
almost unconscious intimation of these same universals as
they form the deep structure of our own nature. We have all
had an experience in which suddenly our mind is afire with
understanding, and the reality around us lights up with meaning. The essential ideas of theosophy can take hold of us in
such moments in which we *know* for ourselves that they are
real and at work all round us. When insight is charged with
such feeling and enthusiasm, it can penetrate into the recesses
of our being at all levels and suffuse our lives and actions.

If we continue to study and contemplate these great
philosophic ideas, they can slowly transform our world view,

even reaching to the unconscious levels where much of this inner picture resides. Slowly, as the various aspects of our nature are brought into harmony with the Ancient Wisdom, we might sense our profound relationship with the universe. This widens our focal setting and we may open to our many rich interconnections and become immersed in the One at all levels of our being. We are then more connected to the world around us through our many interrelations and more attuned to the sacredness of life, the divine essence within all things. Thus we would live more and more in remembrance of the all-encompassing Ground that pervades and sustains all.

If as a species we could come to see ourselves in this light, if we could feel our cosmic underpinnings, we would take our place in the natural order. We would know our identity with each other and with all forms of life and live more nobly, more compassionately. Instead of being concerned primarily with self-centered interest, we would expand into a universal perspective. As the sage is depicted in beautiful old Chinese paintings, we would blend harmoniously into the landscape, contemplating the life of the mountains and the stream. This could transform the world.

Nicholas Roerich, "The Snow Maiden"

Notes

Introduction

1. Albert Einstein, *Ideas and Opinions* (New York: Crown Publishers, Inc., 1954), p. 38.

2. Renée Weber, "The Reluctant Tradition," *Main Currents in Modern Thought,* 31, no. 4 (1975): 105.

3. Ibid., p. 101.

4. Frithjof Schuon, *The Transcendent Unity of Religions,* Peter Townsend, trans., (Wheaton, IL: Theosophical Publishing House, 1984), pp. 3-4.

5. Jacob Needleman, *The Heart of Philosophy,* (New York: Alfred A. Knopf, 1982), p. 162.

6. Weber, "The Reluctant Tradition," p. 99

7. Helena P. Blavatsky, *The Secret Doctrine* (Adyar: Theosophical Publishing House, 1978), 1:316.

8. Ibid., 1:85.

9. Ibid., 4:362.

10. *Letters from the Masters of Wisdom, First Series,* C. Jinarajadasa, ed., (Adyar: Theosophical Publishing House, 1948), p. 2.

11. *The Secret Doctrine,* 1:86

12. Georg Feuerstein, *An Introduction to the Bhagavad Gita,* (Wheaton: Theosophical Publishing House, Quest Books, 1983), p. 86.

13. Sri Krishna Prem and Sri Madhava Ashish, *Man, the Measure of All Things* (Wheaton: Theosophical Publishing House, 1969), p. 15.

14. Schuon, *The Transcendent Unity of Religions,* p. xxxi-ii.

1. The Healing World View

1. Jacob Needleman, *The Heart of Philosophy,* p. 3.

2. Ken Wilber, *The Spectrum of Consciousness* (Wheaton, IL.: Theosophical Publishing House, 1979), p. 150.

3. David Bohm, *Wholeness and the Implicate Order* (London: Routledge and Kegan Paul, 1980), p. xi.

4. Albert Einstein, *Ideas and Questions* (New York: Crown Publishers, Inc., 1954), p. 38.

5. David Bohm, "The Enfolding-Unfolding Universe: A Conversation with David Bohm," by Renée Weber, *Re-Vision*, 1, nos. 3/4 (1978): 48.

6. Stanislav Grof, "Modern Consciousness Research and the Quest for a New Paradigm," *Re-Vision*, 2, no. 1 (1979): 48.

7. C. G. Jung, *Memories, Dreams, Reflections*, ed., Aniela Jaffe, (New York: Random House, 1965), pp. 225-26.

8. Erwin Schroedinger, *My View of the World* (London: Cambridge University Press, 1964), p. 21.

9. *Lankavatara Sutra*.

10. Arthur Koestler, *Darkness at Noon* (New York: Signet Classics, 1961), p. xix.

11. Sun Bear, in Evelyn Eaton, *The Shaman and the Medicine Wheel* (Wheaton: Theosophical Publishing House, 1982), p. 169.

2. Interconnections

1. *Secret Doctrine*, 1:118.

2. Ibid., 1:69.

3. Ibid., 1:115-6.

4. Ibid., 2:359.

5. Ibid., 1:123.

6. H. P. Blavatsky, *Key to Theosophy*, ed., Joy Mills, (Wheaton, Theosophical Publishing House, 1981), p. 50.

7. *Secret Doctrine*, 1:36.

8. Ibid., 2:328.

9. Ibid., 1:179.

10. Guy Murchie, *The Seven Mysteries of Life*, (Boston: Houghton Mifflin, 1981).

11. Fairfield Osborn in Introduction to John Storer, *The Web of Life*, (New York: New American Library, 1972).

12. See Gregory Bateson, *Steps to an Ecology of Mind* (New York: Ballantine Books, 1972).

13. C. G. Jung in Foreword to Jolande Jacobi, *The Psychology of C. G. Jung* (London: Routledge and Kegan Paul, 1968).

14. David Spangler, *Revelations: The Birth of a New Age* (Elgin: Lorian Press, 1979).

3. Holism and Hierarchy

1. Ken Wilber, *The Spectrum of Consciousness, p.* 72.
2. *Secret Doctrine,* 2:329.
3. L. L. Whyte, *Accent on Form* (Westport, CT: Greenwood Press, 1973), p. 53-4.
4. Joseph Needham, *Science and Civilization in China* (London: Cambridge University Press, 1956), vol. 2, p. 582.
5. Teilhard de Chardin, *The Phenomenon of Man* (New York: Harper Torchbooks, 1965), pp. 43-4.
6. Alfred North Whitehead, *Modes of Thought* (New York: Macmillan, 1968).

4. The Transcendent Source

1. Prem and Ashish, *Man, the Measure,* p.154.
2. *Secret Doctrine,* 1:79.
3. Ibid., 1:79.
4. Ibid., 1:83.
5. Ibid., 5:261.
6. Ibid., 1:320.
7. Ibid., 1:142.
8. J. C. Chatterji, *The Wisdom of the Vedas* (Wheaton: Theosophical Publishing House, 1973), p. 25.
9. Fritjof Capra, "An Interview with Fritjof Capra," *Re-Vision,* 4, no. 1 (1981): 45.
10. Lawrence LeShan and Henry Margenau, *Einstein's Space and Van Gogh's Sky* (New York: Macmillan Publishing Co., 1983), pp. 117-8.
11. Fritjof Capra, *The Tao of Physics* (Berkeley: Shambhala Publications, Inc., 1975), p. 211.
12. Ibid., p. 222-3.
13. F. L. Kunz, "From the Unreal to the Real" (privately published paper, 1966).
14. _____, "The Reality of the Non-Material," *Main Currents in Modern Thought,* Retrospective Issue, 1975, p. 20.
15. Capra, *The Tao of Physics,* p. 211.
16. David Bohm, "The Enfolding-Unfolding Universe: A Conversation with David Bohm."

5. The Divinity of Space

1. A. T. Barker, compiler, *The Mahatma Letters* (Adyar: Theosophical Publishing House, 1962), p. 52.

2. Prem and Ashish, *Man, the Measure*, p. 142.

3. Henry Margenau, ed., *Integrative Principles in Modern Thought* (New York: Gordon Breach, 1972), p. 29.

4. Prem and Ashish, *Man, the Measure*, p. 270.

5. *Secret Doctrine*, 1:70.

6. Joseph Campbell, *Hero with a Thousand Faces* (Princeton: Princeton University Press, Bollingen Series XVII), p. 258.

6. The Cosmic Heartbeat

1. Chatterji, *The Wisdom of the Vedas* (see chap. 4, n. 8), p. 14.

2. *Secret Doctrine*, 1:70

3. Ibid., 1:116

4. Ibid., 1:160

5. Fritjof Capra, "Holistic World Views of Physicists and Mystics," *The American Theosophist*, May, 1979.

6. *Mahatma Letters*, p. 55.

7. Garrett Serviss, *The Einstein Theory of Relativity* (New York: E. M Fadman, 1923), p. 48.

8. Capra, *Tao of Physics*, pp. 24-25.

9. *Mahatma Letters*, p. 137.

10. Ibid., pp. 155-56.

11. Capra, *Tao of Physics*, pp. 24-25.

12. *Mahatma Letters*, p. 137.

13. *Secret Doctrine*, 1:125.

14. Ibid., 1:160.

15. Prem and Ashish, *Man the Measure*, p. 73.

16. Ibid., p. 80.

17. Chatterji, *Wisdom of the Vedas*, p. 26.

7. Time and Timelessness

1. *Secret Doctrine*, 1:116.

2. Ibid.

3. Ibid.

4. Ibid.

5. Ibid., 4:183-4.

6. Larry Dossey, *Space, Time and Medicine* (Boulder, Colo.: Shambhala, 1982), chapter 8.

7. Douglas K. Wood, "Even Such is Time," *Re-Vision*, 1, no. 1 (1978): 48.

8. *Secret Doctrine*, 1:110.

9. Ibid., 1:116.

10. Ibid., 1:131.

11. Ibid., 2:136.

12. Ibid., 2:117.

13. Quoted in Dossey, *Space, Time and Medicine*, p. 152.

14. H. S. Margenau, in Preface to L. LeShan, *Toward a General Theory of the Paranormal* (New York, Parapsychology Foundation, 1969).

15. Quoted in Gary Zukav, *The Dancing Wu Lei Masters* (New York, William Morrow and Co., 1979), p. 313.

16. I. K. Taimni, *Man, God and the Universe* (Wheaton: Theosophical Publishing House, 1969), p. 354.

17. Quoted in *The Secret Doctrine*, p. 1:116.

18. Jean Shomoda Bolen, *The Tao of Psychology* (New York: Harper and Row, 1979), p. 7.

19. Ananda K. Coomaraswamy, *Time and Eternity* (Switzerland: Ascona, 1947), p. 71.

20. Prem and Ashish, *Man, the Measure*, p.113.

21. *Secret Doctrine*, 5:482.

22. Prem and Ashish, *Man, the Measure*, p. 55.

23. D. T. Suzuki, in Preface to B. L. Suzuki, *Mahayana Buddhism* (New York: Macmillan, 1969), p. 33.

24. Lama A. Govinda, *Foundations of Tibetan Mysticism* (New York: Samuel Weiser, 1974), p. 116.

25. *Secret Doctrine*, 3:166.

26. Prem and Ashish, *Man, the Measure*, p. 59.

8. The Two in One

1. Capra, *The Tao of Physics*, pp. 24-25.

2. *Secret Doctrine*, 1:81.

3. Ibid., 1:109

4. Ibid., 1:80.

5. Ibid., 2:42.

6. Ibid., 1:83.

7. Ibid., 1:94.

8. Dossey, *Space, Time, and Medicine*, Chapter 8.

9. *The Secret Doctrine*, 1:317.

10. Erich Jantsch, *The Self-Organizing Universe* (Elmsford, N.Y.: Pergamon Press, 1980), p. 40.

11. *Secret Doctrine*, 1:320.

12. Ibid., 1:80.

13. Alan Watts, *Two Hands of God* (New York: Macmillan, 1969).

14. Prem and Ashish, *Man the Measure*, p. 80.

15. Watts, *Two Hands of God*.

16. Capra, *The Tao of Physics*, p. 141.

17. Wilber, *The Spectrum of Consciousness*, p. 40.

9. Rhythm and Cycles

1. *Secret Doctrine*, p. 1:70.

2. Ibid., 1:176.

3. Prem and Ashish, *Man the Measure*, p. 50.

4. Emily B. Sellon, "Some Principles of Theosophy," unpublished paper.

5. Lama Anagarika Govinda, *Foundations of Tibetan Mysticism* (York Beach, ME: Samuel Weiser, 1982), pp. 151.

6. Ibid., p. 151.

7. Helena P. Blavatsky, *Isis Unveiled*, in *Collected Writings* (Wheaton: Theosophical Publishing House, 1972) vol. 1, p. 388-90.

8. *Secret Doctrine*, 3:444.

9. Prem and Ashish, *Man, the Measure*, p. 298.

10. *Secret Doctrine*, 3:90.

11. Dane Rudhyar, *The Pulse of Life* (Berkeley: Shambhala Publications, 1970) p. 16.

12. Alan Watts, *The Two Hands of God.*

13. *Secret Doctrine*, 1:82.

14. Henry D. Thoreau, *The Natural Man, A Thoreau Anthology*, eds. R. Epstein and S. Phillips (Wheaton: Theosophical Publishing House, 1978), p. 69.

10. Divine Mind

1. *Secret Doctrine*, 1:80.

2. Ibid., 1:81.

3. Albert Einstein, *The World as I See It* (New York: Wisdom Library, 1979), p. 5.

4. Quoted in Prem and Ashish, *Man the Measure*, p. 149.

5. Ibid., p. 100.

6. *Secret Doctrine*, 1:122.

7. Ibid., 1:148.

8. Prem and Ashish, *Man the Measure*, p. 13.

9. *Secret Doctrine*, 3:38.

10. Prem and Ashish, *Man the Measure*, p. 138.

11. Marjorie Senechal, "Symmetry, the Principle of Order," in M. Senechal and G. Fleck, eds., *Patterns of Symmetry* (Amherst: University of Massachusetts Press, 1977), p. 95.

12. F. L. Kunz, "On the Symmetry Principles," in *Order in the Universe* (New York: The Foundation for Integrative Education, 1967).

13. *Secret Doctrine,* 5:185.

14. For a detailed discussion of the Platonic solids, see Gordon Plummer, *The Mathematics of the Cosmic Mind* (Wheaton, IL: Theosophical Publishing House, 1982).

15. G. C. Amstutz, "Symmetry in Nature and Art," in *Order in the Universe.*

16. Karl Pribram, *"What the Fuss is All About,"* in *Re-Vision* 1, nos., 3/4: 17-18.

17. Ibid., p. 15.

18. Hermann Weyl, *Symmetry* (Princeton: Princeton University Press, 1973), pp. 6-7.

19. *Secret Doctrine,* 5:533.

20. Prem and Ashish, *Man the Measure,* p. 113.

21. *Secret Doctrine,* 3:37.

22. Ibid., 1:304.

23. Loren Eiseley, "Notes of an Alchemist."

24. Prem and Ashish, *Man the Measure,* p. 138.

11. Sevenfold Illusion

1. LeShan and Margenau, *Einstein's Space* (see n. 9, chap. 6), p. 21.

2. *Secret Doctrine,* 4:204.

3. Prem and Ashish, *Man, the Measure,* p. 65.

4. Bernard Grad, "Some Biological Effects of the Laying On of Hands," in *Journal of the American Society for Psychological Research,* 5, no. 2: 95-126.

5. J. Taylor, *Superminds* (London: Macmillan, 1975).

6. L. Day and G. De La Warr, *Matter in the Making* (London: Vincent Stuart Publishers, 1966), p. 8-9.

7. Rupert Sheldrake, *A New Science of Life* (Los Angeles: J. P. Tarcher, 1982).

8. William Tiller, "New Field, New Laws," in John White and S. Krippner, eds. *Future Science,* (Garden City: Doubleday, 1977), p. 60.

9. William Tiller in Introduction to H. Motoyama, *Science and the Evolution of Consciousness* (Brookline, MA: Autumn Press, 1978), p. 9.

10. Tiller, "New Fields," p. 60.

11. Ibid.

12. *Secret Doctrine,* 1:83.

13. H. P. Blavatsky, "Transactions of the Blavatsky Lodge," in *Collected Writings,* vol. X, p. 335.

14. *Secret Doctrine,* 1:331.

15. Ibid., 1:317.

16. Prem and Ashish, *Man, the Measure,* p. 147.

17. *Secret Doctrine,* 1:332.

18. Ravi Ravindra, "Perceptions in Physics and Yoga," *Re-Vision,* 3, no. 1: 37.

12. Progressive Development

1. *Secret Doctrine,* 3:177.

2. Ibid., 1:91.

3. Ibid., 1:320.

4. G. R. Taylor, *The Great Evolution Mystery* (New York: Harper & Row, 1983), p. 202.

5. See "Evolution and Recapitulation," in *The Life Process* (Wheaton, IL: Theosophical Society in America, Dept. of Education, n.d.).

6. D'Arcy Thompson, *On Growth and Form,* (Cambridge: Cambridge University Press, 1952), p. 1094.

7. Stephan Jay Gould, *The Panda's Thumb* (New York: W. W. Norton & Co., 1980).

8. *Secret Doctrine,* 1:317.

9. Ibid., 1:69.

10. Ibid., 3:96.

11. Ibid., 4:224.

12. Ibid., 3:97.

13. Ibid., 3:196.

14. Ibid., 3:187.

15. Ibid., 4:116.

16. Ibid., 3:15.

17. Jantsch, *The Self-Organizing Universe* (see chap. 8, n. 10), p. 3.

18. *Secret Doctrine,* 3:177.

19. Ibid., 1:235.

20. Le Comte du Nouy, *Human Destiny* (Darby, PA: Arden Library, 1981).

21. Oliver Wendell Holmes, "Chambered Nautilus."

13. Karma

1. *Secret Doctrine,* 2:361.

2. H. P. Blavatsky, *The Key to Theosophy,* Joy Mills, ed. (Wheaton, IL: Theosophical Publishing House, 1981).

3. *Secret Doctrine,* 2:359.

4. Ibid., 3:306.

5. Ibid., 2:360.

6. H. P. Blavatksy, *Key to Theosophy* (see chap. 2, n. 6), p. 121.

7. *Secret Doctrine*, 2:368.
8. *Key to Theosophy*, p. 124.
9. *Secret Doctrine*, 3:306.
10. *Key to Theosophy*, p. 124.
11. Prem and Ashish, *Man the Measure*, p. 210.
12. *Secret Doctrine*, 2:367.
13. Ibid., 3:60.
14. Ibid., 2:362.
15. Ibid., 2:366.
16. *Key to Theosophy*, p. 16.
17. *Secret Doctrine*, 2:364.
18. Ibid., 2:365.
19. *Key to Theosophy*, p.121.
20. Prem and Ashish, *Man, the Measure*, p. 114-5.
21. *Secret Doctrine*, 2:369.
22. Mabel Collins, *Light on the Path* (Pasadena: Theosophical University Press, 1976), p. 88.

14. The Self and Its Spheres

1. William James, quoted in Ken Wilber, *Spectrum of Consciousness* (see chap. 3, n. 1), p. 15.
2. *Secret Doctrine*, 5:362.
3. E. B. Sellon, "Some Fundamentals of Theosophy," seminar handout.
4. *Secret Doctrine*, 5:523.
5. Wilbur Schramm, *The Process and Effects of Mass Communication* (Champaign: University of Illinois Press, 1955).
6. Wilber, *Spectrum of Consciousness*, p. 20.
7. Ibid., 149-50.
8. Govinda, *Foundations of Tibetan Mysticism* (see chap. 9, n. 5), p. 74.
9. Ibid., p. 74.
10. Rollo May, *Existence* (New York: Basic Books, 1958), p. 75.
11. Ibid., p. 74.
12. *Secret Doctrine*, 3:89.
13. William James in John J. McDermott, *The Writings of William James* (New York: Random House, Modern Library, 1968), p. 155.
14. V. K. Chari, *Whitman in the Light of Vedantic Mysticism* (Lincoln: University of Nebraska Press, 1964), p. 27.
15. Albert Einstein, *Ideas and Opinions* (New York: Crown, 1954).
16. Brian Josephson, quoted in *Omni*, June, 1982.
17. Chari, *Vedantic Mysticism*, p. 27.

18. I. K. Taimni, *The Way of Self-Discovery* (Wheaton, IL: Theosophical Publishing House, 1970), p. 179.

19. Ibid., p. 168.

15. Self-Transformation

1. Hellmut Wilhelm, *Change* (New York: Harper and Row, 1960), p. 19.

2. Mabel Collins, *Light on the Path,* (Wheaton, IL: Theosophical Publishing House, 1970), p. 20.

3. Taimni, *A Way of Self-Discovery,* p. 166.

4. H. P. Blavatsky, *The Voice of the Silence* (Wheaton, IL: Theosophical Publishing House, 1973), p. 42.

5. Virginia Burden, *The Process of Intuition,* (Wheaton, IL: Theosophical Publishing House, 1975), p.83.

6. P. W. Martin, *An Experiment in Depth* (London: Routledge & Kegan Paul, 1967), p. 277.

7. Lama Govinda, *Foundations of Tibetan Mysticism,* p. 75.

8. T. S. Eliot, "Little Gidding," in *Four Quartets.*

9. *Secret Doctrine,* 3:106.

10. Lama Govinda, *Foundations of Tibetan Mysticism,* p. 75.

11. Ibid., p. 75.

12. Thomas Keefe, *Journal of Contemporary Psychology,* 10:16-24.

13. Blavatsky, *Voice of the Silence,* p. 58.

14. Ibid., p. 38.

15. *The Mahatma Letters* (see chap. 5, n. 1), p. 311.

16. Man the Microcosm

1. *Secret Doctrine,* 1:317

2. Annie Besant, *The Pedigree of Man* (Adyar: Theosophical Publishing House, 1943), p. 22.

3. *Secret Doctrine,* 5:419.

4. Needleman, *The Heart of Philosophy* (see Intro., n. 5), p. 105.

Index

Picture Credits

The author is grateful for permission to reprint the following pictures:

Page 44 – From Raymond F. and Lila K. Piper, *Cosmic Art* (New York: Hawthorn Books, 1975), by permission of Ingo Swann, editor.

Page 52 – Courtesy of NASA.

Page 92 – Christine Majul.

Page 96 – Francis Brunel, Paris, France.

Page 106– Casimir Tomala.

Page 113– Courtesy of NASA.

Page 113– Michael Sellon.

Page 135– From H. E. Huntley, *The Divine Proportion* (New York: Dover Publications, 1970), by permission of the publisher.

Page 179– From C. W. Leadbeater, *The Masters and the Path,* (Adyar: Theosophical Publishing House, 1925), by permission of the publisher.

Page 184– By permission of Dr. Svetoslav Roerich.